LÜBECK

Fotografien von / *Photographs by*
KAREN MEYER-REBENTISCH

LÜBECK

Texte von / *Texts by*
JAN ZIMMERMANN

JUNIUS

INHALT

6	Vorwort	
10	**St. Petri**	Erster Auftritt: Holstentor und Salzspeicher – unbekannte Blicke – lichte Weite
16	**St. Marien**	Die „Mutter der Backsteingotik" – imposantes Gewölbe – warmes Farbspiel
22	**Das Rathaus**	Architektur-Puzzle – Repräsentation – von Bürgermeistern und Bürgerschaft
36	**Rippen- und Querstraßen**	Spaziergang mit Schaufensterbummel in der Hüxstraße – Gastronomie und Kultur
46	**Die Rückseiten der Stadt**	Spielplätze für Sport, Kreativität und Kultur – und ein Kunstatelier
50	**Backstein über Backstein**	Der Baustoff der großen Kirchen und Gebäude – das Gesicht der Stadt
58	**Reformierte Kirche**	Ruhe und Klarheit – Konzentration auf das Wesentliche
60	**Wohnen einst und heute**	Mittelalterliche Diele – wie Bürger wohnten – Althaussanierung trifft Kunst im Denkmal
66	**Überliefertes Handwerk**	Traditionsbetriebe der Stadt – Rotter Glas und Niederegger
70	**Schiffer und Schiffe**	Schiffergesellschaft, die Viermastbark *Passat* und die „großen Pötte"
80	**Am Strand von Travemünde**	Wegfahren, ankommen, sitzen, schauen
84	**Blühendes Lübeck**	Rosenblüten in sonnigen Altstadtgassen – Freude für Augen und Nase
88	**Höfe und Gänge**	Versteckt, nicht unzugänglich – idyllische Plätze zum Wohnen
92	**Dicht am Wasser**	Kunst-Tankstelle, Sprung ins Nass und bester Platz am Wasser
102	**St. Katharinen**	Kirche ohne Turm – zweistöckiger Chor – der Toten gedenken
108	**Lübecks Untergrund**	Besuch in mittelalterlichen Gewölbekellern
110	**Die Synagoge**	Das jüdische Gotteshaus – einst geschändet, heute prachtvoll und frisch renoviert
112	**Das St. Annen-Museum**	Altäre und Kirchenkunst
116	**Europäisches Hansemuseum**	Als Lübeck die Königin der Hanse war
122	**Themen der Zeitgeschichte**	Das 20. Jahrhundert: Lübecker Märtyrer – Willy-Brandt-Haus – Industriegeschichte
128	**Am Stadthafen**	Industriedenkmäler und Spuren des früheren Hafenbetriebs – ein maritimes Freilichtmuseum
144	**St. Jakobi**	Eine barocke Seefahrerkirche – und ein moderner Gedenkort
150	**Musik erklingt**	Klassische Orgel, Bass und Beats – eine lebendige Musikszene
160	**Welt der Bücher**	Literaturnobelpreisträger, gelehrte Pastoren und Bücher für alle
170	**Kunst von heute und damals**	Vis-à-vis – das Kunsthaus und das Behnhaus
176	**Wege in die Stadt**	Die Stadt ist eine Insel – durch Tore und über Brücken in die Altstadt
182	**Herbst im Grünen**	Die Wallanlagen – der Schulgarten – grüne Inseln in der Stadt
188	**Der Dom**	Mächtige Altstadtkirche mit Doppelturm
192	**Dunst und Dämmerung**	Im herbstlichen Nebel und zur Blauen Stunde
198	**St. Aegidien**	Die kleinste Altstadtkirche – reich ausgestattet
204	**Weihnachtsstadt**	Advent in den Kirchen – Kunsthandwerk und bunte Lichter
212	**Bei Eis und Schnee**	Wintervergnügen auf dem Rathausmarkt – Ruhe am Wasser

have been revitalised and provide a mix of residential, commercial, and recreational spaces – an urban development that Lübeck shares with many other seaports. The recently built European Hansemuseum has an accessible rooftop terrace that offers panoramic views of the historic port. It is nestled against the medieval Burgkloster (Dominican friary), enabling visitors to bridge centuries in just a few steps. "Everything is 'close by' in Lübeck", wrote Thomas Mann. Travemünde may be a bit farther away, but it is beautifully situated on the Baltic Sea, which more than makes up for the distance.

The photographs of Karen Meyer-Rebentisch document Lübeck, its people, and their way of life. After living in Berlin, she decided to make Lübeck her home in 1993. She has dedicated the last ten years to exploring and discovering the city through her lens with boundless curiosity about places, people, art, and culture. As a keen cultural scholar with an interest in the history of this Hanseatic city, she has an understanding of its layers of time and the history encased in every brick. She finds it particularly appealing to live in a place where history is so tangible. Not only that of the Hanseatic period and the Middle Ages, but also the more recent history of the twentieth century – the Third Reich, World War II, and the decades when Lübeck was a border city to East Germany.

But – and that is what distinguishes this book from other photographic portraits of Lübeck – buildings don't tell the full story. Images need people to show life in the city as it is today. Lübeck has museums but is not itself a museum. That is amply demonstrated by the images of the Altstadt, which is enjoying a new lease on life. Brick, water, and light – these are the three themes Karen Meyer-Rebentisch has chosen for her photographic study of Lübeck. The weathered bricks of the churches in the Altstadt tell of people who lived here hundreds of years ago and built their city and places of worship. The churches have been a powerful force in shaping the urban landscape of Lübeck; without them, the city would look very different. A few years ago, Karen Meyer-Rebentisch initiated the Sieben Türme calendar, the proceeds of which go towards renovating the churches of the Altstadt, and every year she succeeds in showing the city's great churches in a new light.

Being a photographer, Karen Meyer-Rebentisch understands that light can work wonders. Mood depends on light, and it can make one and the same place appear so different. Places can even take on an entirely new appearance depending on the weather and time of day: the bright light of the sun, the soft glow of dawn, a storm brewing, or dense autumn fog. For her, as a light chaser, urban photography is particularly challenging; she has to study the light, anticipate it, track it down, patiently wait for it, follow it and finally, catch the perfect moment. Sometimes she has to hurry, and adrenaline floods her body when she knows she is on the right track. That makes her pedal faster on her red bike, driven by the worry that the light might escape her. She is a committed cyclist because biking has the right speed; she can still take in her surroundings and stop quickly if she needs to.

Water influences Lübeck in so many ways. The port enabled the city near the Baltic Sea to become Queen of the Hanse, and the Trave River links Lübeck with its hinterland. Water surrounds the Altstadt on all sides and contributes considerably to the quality of life in the city. One doesn't have to go far to find a spot on a riverbank to relax and take in the slow flow of the Trave, to watch people enjoying water sports on the Wakenitz, or to take a refreshing plunge at one of the many bathing spots. Many people go on holiday to faraway places to stroll along the waterfront and sit by the water – in Lübeck that's just part of everyday life. And if time allows, a day on the Baltic Sea is like a mini holiday. That's something that always makes Karen Meyer-Rebentisch happy.

Jan Zimmermann

BRICK, WATER, AND LIGHT

"What does this mean. – What – does this mean…"
Thus begins Buddenbrooks, Thomas Mann's epic novel set in Lübeck. It was an important city in the Middle Ages, as evidenced by its magnificent churches, the Rathaus and the two remaining city gates. It is a medieval city built on an island – the Altstadt (old city) is still surrounded by water. Only a few remnants of the city wall and ramparts remain, but water still abounds, and its presence influences all aspects of life in Lübeck. Usually in a good way, as the abundance of water provides beautiful views and many leisure opportunities, and combined with Lübeck's many parks, it makes it a very liveable city. But an island city has its drawbacks too, such as when the waters of the Trave and Wakenitz rivers act as natural barriers, and dilapidated bridges bring traffic to a standstill.

Lübeck is still a city, though no longer a major one. Much of what makes an urban centre important is still concentrated in the historic Altstadt – from municipal offices to shops to restaurants and cafés, and above all cultural venues. Museums, libraries, theatres, and galleries are spread over a network of streets laid out 800 years ago and hardly changed since. The layout of the streets may have remained the same, but their elevation hasn't. Archaeologists in Lübeck must dig several metres underground to find traces of the early settlement. Recent excavations have uncovered finds from the early decades of the city's history: the foundations of buildings, cellars, and staircases from the late twelfth century. One of the most surprising discoveries was that fired bricks were already in use at that time to build houses. Archaeologists had previously assumed that in the period around 1180, bricks were manufactured for use only in large construction projects, such as the cathedral and the city walls. However, that assumption was corrected when a staircase belonging to a twelfth-century private house was excavated in the city's oldest quarter between St. Mary's Church and the River Trave.

Brick and wood are extremely durable materials, and they are still a common sight in the Altstadt. In particular, the firewalls of old houses often date from the Middle Ages, and restoration works frequently reveal wall paintings beneath the plaster. The oldest roof trusses date from the thirteenth century – an example of truly sustainable construction. Lübeck does not have catacombs, but it does have some medieval vaulted cellars that were discovered below more recently built houses. These invisible layers are a big part of the city's architectural heritage, which comprises so much more than majestic churches, the Rathaus, and the Holsten Gate.

Even if the Altstadt has lost some of its appeal for locals – because getting there by car is a hassle compared to shopping at malls on the outskirts – it is by no means a museum inhabited exclusively by the owners of historic houses. Fourteen thousand people live on the island, among them many students. Lübeck does not have a traditional university, but it does have several other institutions of higher learning, such as the Academy of Music, the University of Lübeck (a research university with a focus on medicine), the Technical University of Applied Sciences, and Germany's federal police academy. These institutions attract young people from across Germany and many other countries, bringing new life to the Altstadt, where a wide variety of restaurants, bars and cafés have opened. Given the vacancy rate in centrally located high streets, it is clear that there is no stopping change. While small, independently owned shops in old buildings thrive, large spaces in commercial buildings from the post-war era sit vacant. In the 1970s, Lübeck was a city of industry and trade; today, more than a fifth of its workforce is occupied in the health sector. The city has always experienced change, but this has accelerated in the digital age.

Most of the western waterfront of the Altstadt has been cleared of parked cars in recent years, and the new square, Drehbrückenplatz, has become a popular meeting place. The old, mostly unused docks

noch vom Hafenbetrieb beansprucht, erwachen zu neuem Leben, mit einer Mischung aus Arbeiten, Wohnen und Freizeit. Eine Entwicklung, die Lübeck mit vielen anderen Hafenstädten verbindet. Wer auf der frei zugänglichen Dachterrasse des noch jungen Europäischen Hansemuseums steht, hat einen weiten Blick auf den historischen Hafen – und gleichzeitig das mittelalterliche Burgkloster im Rücken: Wenige Meter überbrücken Jahrhunderte. „In Lübeck ist ja alles ‚in der Nähe'", wie schon Thomas Mann resümierte. Nur Travemünde liegt ein wenig weiter, dafür aber umso schöner an der Ostsee.

Karen Meyer-Rebentisch begleitet Lübeck und das Leben hier mit ihrer Kamera. 1993 hat sie, aus Berlin kommend, Lübeck zum Lebensort gewählt. Seit einem Jahrzehnt erkundet und entdeckt sie die Stadt mit dem Blick durch das Objektiv, immer neugierig auf Orte und Menschen, auf Kunst und Kultur. Als in der zeitgeschichtlichen Forschung der Hansestadt engagierte Kulturwissenschaftlerin hat sie einen Sinn für die Zeitschichten von Orten und jene Geschichtlichkeit, die in jedem (Back-)Stein enthalten ist. Und als Historikerin spricht es sie besonders tief an, an einem Ort zu leben, an dem ihr Geschichte ständig begegnet. Nicht nur die der Hansezeit und des Mittelalters, sondern auch die Zeitgeschichte des 20. Jahrhunderts, mit dem Dritten Reich, dem Zweiten Weltkrieg und den Jahrzehnten Lübecks als Großstadt an der Grenze zur DDR.

Aber – und das unterscheidet dieses Buch von anderen fotografischen Porträts der Stadt – Bauten allein können nicht alles erzählen. Es braucht die Menschen im Bild, um die lebendige Gegenwart abzubilden. Lübeck hat Museen, aber ist kein Museum: Das zeigen die Fotos der Altstadtstraßen, die sich neu erfinden. Steine, Wasser und Licht: Das sind die drei Themen, die Karen Meyer-Rebentisch als Gegenstand ihrer fotografischen Arbeit in Lübeck hervorhebt. Die verwitterten Ziegel der Altstadtkirchen erzählen von Menschen, die hier vor Hunderten von Jahren lebten und sich ihre Stadt erbauten, ihre Gotteshäuser. Die Kirchen prägen kraftvoll das Bild Lübecks, ohne sie hätte die Stadt eine ganz andere Anmutung. Als Erfinderin des Sieben-Türme-Kalenders, dessen Erträge der Sanierung der Altstadtkirchen zugutekommen, hat Karen Meyer-Rebentisch die großen Kirchen in den letzten Jahren aus immer neuen Perspektiven porträtiert.

Licht ist für Karen Meyer-Rebentisch als Fotografin das Wichtigste überhaupt. Denn es kann zaubern. Wie sehr sich eine Stimmung verändert, je nachdem ob die Sonne scheint oder es dämmert, dunkle Wolken aufziehen oder gar herbstlicher Nebel – ein und derselbe Ort kann so unterschiedlich wirken und immer wieder wie neu erscheinen! Das Licht zu erkunden und vorauszuahnen, es aufzuspüren oder geduldig zu erwarten, ihm zu folgen und es einzufangen, das ist für sie als Jägerin des Lichts die besondere Herausforderung in der Stadtfotografie. Manchmal muss es dann schnell gehen und Adrenalin flutet ihren Körper, wenn sie glaubt, auf dem richtigen Weg zu sein. Es lässt sie fester in die Pedale ihres roten Fahrrades treten, getrieben von der Sorge, dass ihr das Licht davoneilen könnte. Auf zwei Rädern ist sie aus Überzeugung unterwegs – weil es genau das richtige Tempo ist, um noch offen zu sein, schnell anhalten zu können.

Wasser – es prägt Lübeck von vielen Seiten: Der Hafen ließ die Stadt nahe der Ostsee zur Königin der Hanse werden, die Trave verband sie mit dem Binnenland. Das Wasser umgibt die Altstadt von allen Seiten und macht einen ganz wesentlichen Teil der Lebensqualität in der Stadt aus: Man muss nicht weit gehen, um sich an irgendein Ufer zu setzen und zur Ruhe zu kommen. Dem ruhigen Dahinfließen der Trave oder den Wassersportlern auf der Wakenitz zuzusehen oder selbst an einer der vielen Badestellen einzutauchen und sich zu erfrischen. Am Wasser zu flanieren, am Wasser zu sitzen – viele Menschen fahren für den Urlaub an weit entfernte Orte, um das zu erleben –, in Lübeck ist es Alltag und zugleich eine kleine Auszeit. Und wenn ein wenig länger Zeit ist: Ein Tag an der Ostsee ist wie ein kurzer Urlaub. Und das macht den Genussmenschen Karen Meyer-Rebentisch immer wieder glücklich.

Jan Zimmermann

STEINE,
WASSER,
LICHT

»Was ist das. – Was – ist das ...« – so beginnen die *Buddenbrooks*, Lübecks Stadtroman von Thomas Mann. Ja, was ist das, diese Stadt nahe der Ostsee? Im Mittelalter eine Metropole, wovon die imposanten Kirchen, das Rathaus und die Stadttore immer noch zeugen. Eine mittelalterliche Großstadt, deren Grenzen durch das Wasser rund um die Altstadt auch heute noch sichtbar sind. Von der Stadtmauer und den Wällen sind nur Reste vorhanden, das Wasser aber ist überall – und für das Leben in Lübeck von größter Bedeutung. Meist in gutem Sinn, um an und auf ihm die Freizeit zu genießen, den Blick zu weiten und um zusammen mit den vielen Grünanlagen für ein gutes Klima zu sorgen. In schlechtem Sinn, wenn sich das Wasser der beiden Flüsse Trave und Wakenitz als Hindernis für den Verkehr erweist und marode Brücken ihn stocken lassen.

Großstadt ist Lübeck auch heute, wenn auch keine mehr von den ganz großen. Noch immer konzentriert sich vieles von dem, was ein Oberzentrum bietet, in der historischen Altstadt. Von der Verwaltung über das Einkaufen bis zur Gastronomie und vor allem der Kultur. Museen, Bibliothek, Theater und Galerien verteilen sich in einem Straßennetz, das sich vor 800 Jahren entwickelt und seitdem kaum verändert hat. Zumindest der Verlauf der Straßen ist geblieben, nicht aber ihr Höhenniveau: Die Lübecker Archäologie muss sich deshalb mehrere Meter in den Untergrund arbeiten, um die frühe Besiedlung zu dokumentieren. Bei Grabungen der letzten Jahre gelang es, Funde aus den ersten Jahrzehnten der Stadtgeschichte zu machen: Hausfundamente, Keller und Treppen aus der zweiten Hälfte des 12. Jahrhunderts. Eines der überraschenden Ergebnisse war, dass die gebrannten Ziegel schon im Hausbau dieser frühen Zeit Verwendung fanden. Bis dahin hatte man angenommen, dass der Backstein um 1180 nur für die großen Bauvorhaben Dom und Stadtmauer hergestellt wurde; eine ausgegrabene, profane Kellertreppe im „Gründungsviertel" zwischen St. Marien und der Trave aus derselben Zeit korrigierte diese Vermutung.

Backstein und Holz als äußerst nachhaltige Baustoffe machen auch heute noch einen großen Teil der Altstadt aus. Vor allem die Brandmauern der alten, meist denkmalgeschützten Häuser stammen oft noch aus dem Mittelalter, und bei Sanierungen tauchen unter dem Putz immer wieder bislang nicht entdeckte Wandmalereien auf. Die ältesten Dachstühle datieren aus dem 13. Jahrhundert – nachhaltigeres Bauen geht nicht. Lübeck hat keine Katakomben, aber unter manchen jüngeren Häusern verstecken sich mittelalterliche Gewölbekeller. Dieses vielschichtig Unsichtbare macht einen großen Teil des architektonischen Erbes der Stadt aus, das aus weit mehr als den großen Kirchen, dem Rathaus und dem Holstentor besteht.

Auch wenn die Altstadt für einige Einheimische heute kein automatischer Anziehungspunkt mehr ist – weil das Einkaufen auf der grünen Wiese einfacher ist, weil die Zufahrt zur Altstadt mit dem Auto Nerven kosten kann –, so ist sie keineswegs ein Museum, das nur von den Besitzern sanierter historischer Häuser belebt wird. 14 000 Menschen wohnen auf der Altstadtinsel, darunter auch viele Studierende. Lübeck hat keine Volluniversität; aber die Musikhochschule, die (medizinische) Universität zu Lübeck, die Technische Hochschule und die Bundespolizeiakademie ziehen junge Menschen aus Deutschland und anderen Ländern in die Stadt. Das ist in den letzten Jahren vor allem dort zu sehen, wo sich Altstadtstraßen durch neue, vielfältige gastronomische Angebote herausputzen. Angesichts des Leerstands in zentralen Einkaufsstraßen ist es offensichtlich, dass sich ein Wandlungsprozess fortsetzen wird: Während kleine, unabhängige Läden in alten Häusern erfolgreich sind, warten große Leerflächen in Geschäftshäusern der Nachkriegszeit vergeblich auf Mietwillige. In den 1970er Jahren war Lübeck eine Industrie- und Handelsstadt, heute arbeitet über ein Fünftel der sozialversicherungspflichtig Beschäftigten in Unternehmen der Gesundheitswirtschaft. Wandel war schon immer ein Charakteristikum der Stadt, nur hat sich dessen Geschwindigkeit im Online-Zeitalter erhöht.

Die westliche Wasserkante der Altstadt ist in den letzten Jahren zu einem wesentlichen Teil von parkenden Autos befreit worden, der neue Drehbrückenplatz hat sich in kurzer Zeit zum beliebten Treffpunkt entwickelt. Die alten Kaistrecken im Stadthafen, heute kaum

CONTENTS

8		*Preface*
10	**St. Peter's Church**	*First impressions: Holsten Gate and the salt warehouses – unexpected views – clear spans*
16	**St. Mary's Church**	*The "Mother of brick Gothic" – impressive vaulted ceilings – a warm play of colours*
22	**The Rathaus**	*An architectural jigsaw puzzle – pomp and prestige – mayors and city governors*
36	**Criss-cross streets**	*Window-shopping on Hüxstrasse – gastronomy and culture*
46	**The fun side of the city**	*Playgrounds for sport, creativity and culture – and an artists' studio*
50	**Brick on brick**	*The stuff of which mighty churches are built – the face of the city*
58	**Reformed Church**	*Calm and clarity – focus on the essential*
60	**Styles of living, then and now**	*Medieval hallway – bourgeois homes – restoration meets art in a historic building*
66	**Timeless craftsmanship**	*Rotter Glas and Niederegger – traditional crafts in Lübeck*
70	**Ships and skippers**	*Historical Skippers' Society, the four-masted barque Passat, and the 'big tubs'*
80	**On Travemünde strand**	*Leaving, arriving, sitting, watching*
84	**Lübeck in bloom**	*Rose blossoms abound in sunny Altstadt lanes – a delight for the nose and the eye*
88	**Courtyards and alleys**	*Hidden, yet accessible – idyllic places to live*
92	**Close to the water**	*Cultural Filling Station, a plunge into water, and the best spot on the waterfront*
102	**St. Catherine's**	*A church without a steeple – a two-storey choir – remembering the dead*
108	**Subterranean Lübeck**	*A visit to medieval vaulted cellars*
110	**The synagogue**	*The Jewish house of worship – once desecrated, now resplendent and freshly renovated*
112	**St. Anne's Museum**	*Altars and church art*
116	**European Hansemuseum**	*When Lübeck was Queen of the Hanseatic League*
122	**Themes in contemporary history**	*The 20th Century: Lübeck's martyrs – Willy-Brandt-Haus – industrial history*
128	**On the docks**	*Industrial monuments and relics of a once-busy port – an open-air maritime museum*
144	**St. James' Church**	*A baroque seafarers' church – and a modern place of remembrance*
150	**The sound of music**	*Classical organ, bass and beats – a lively music scene*
160	**The world of books**	*Nobel literature laureates, learned pastors and books for all*
170	**Art then and now**	*Vis-à-vis – the Kunsthaus and the Behn House*
176	**Pathways into the city**	*The city on an island – entering the Altstadt through gates and over bridges*
182	**Autumnal moods**	*The landscaped ramparts – the school garden – green oases in the city*
188	**The cathedral**	*Mighty twin-towered church*
192	**Misty twilight**	*Autumn mist and the blue hour*
198	**St. Aegidien's Church**	*The smallest church in the Altstadt – lavishly furnished*
204	**The city at Christmas**	*Advent in the churches – artisan crafts and bright lights*
212	**Ice and snow**	*Winter delights on Rathaus square – tranquility by the water*

VORHANG AUF / *THE CURTAIN RAISER*

Der Blick von Westen, am besten bei später Sonne – das ist die Perspektive auf die große Bühne der Hansestadt. Im Vordergrund stellt sich das Holstentor in Pose, hinter sich scharrt es die Baudenkmäler aus Backstein: die sechsgiebelige Gruppe der Salzspeicher und dahinter den Turm von St. Petri, von dessen Plattform aus die Altstadtinsel mit einem Rundblick zu erfassen ist.

The view from the west, preferably just before sunset, offers an impressive panorama of Lübeck's mise en scène. In the foreground is the iconic Holsten Gate (Holstentor), just behind it a row of six historic red-brick salt warehouses, and rising behind them, the tower of St. Peter's Church (St. Petri), from whose viewing platform visitors can enjoy a commanding view of the old city.

TÜRME THRONEN / *MAJESTIC SPIRES*

St. Petri, erkennbar an den vier kleinen Ecktürmen, erhebt sich auf dem Stadthügel über der Obertrave und erhält aus dieser Perspektive den Vortritt vor St. Marien. Von Schwans Hof in der Hartengrube aus erscheint St. Petri wie ein Wachturm. Nicht zu Unrecht, melden doch noch bis ins 19. Jahrhundert Turmwächter, wenn ein Feuer ausgebrochen war.

St. Peter's is immediately recognizable by the four smaller spires at the corners of the main steeple. It is situated on a slight incline overlooking the Trave River and, from this perspective, slightly upstages nearby St. Mary's Church (Marienkirche). Seen from the secluded Schwans Hof alley at the heart of the Altstadt, St. Peter's looks like a watchtower; appropriately so, as watchmen were stationed here until the 19th century to warn of possible fires.

LICHTE WEITE / *A CLEAR SPAN*

Mit der Zerstörung 1942 verlor St. Petri seine Eigenständigkeit als Kirchspiel, seine Gemeinde und seine Funktion. Erst in den 1980er Jahren waren Sicherung und Wiederaufbau abgeschlossen – nach düsteren Jahrzehnten aber ist die fünfschiffige Hallenkirche seitdem so licht wie keine andere Altstadtkirche. Sie dient als Raum für neue theologische Konzepte, für Kunst und Kultur.

Following extensive damage in an Allied bombing raid in 1942, St. Peter's ceased to function as a parish church. It wasn't until the 1980s that the building was fully restored and secured. After several gloomy decades, this five-aisle hall church is now the most expansive and brightly lit of Lübeck's historic churches. Today it serves as a space for various religious, artistic and cultural events.

ST. MARIEN IN BLAU
ST. MARY'S IN BLUE

Wer Abstand nimmt von der Altstadt und auf der Eric-Warburg-Brücke stehend über Trave und Hafen schaut, erhält ein die Epochen vereinendes Bild mit St. Marien als überragendem Bauwerk. Eine „gotische Mondnacht" findet sich bei Heinrich Mann, in seinem Roman *Professor Unrat*: Rechts leuchtet das passende Foto auf, der Mond eingerahmt von den gotischen Türmen.

If we leave the Altstadt behind and take in the view from the Eric Warburg Bridge over the Trave and the Lübeck port, the scene incorporates several different eras of Lübeck life. Central to the scene is the imposing figure of St. Mary's Church. The writer Heinrich Mann described a 'Gothic moonlight' in his novel Professor Unrat. The photo to the right captures this motif perfectly, with the moon framed by the twin Gothic spires of St. Mary's.

18 ST. MARIEN

GOTISCHE GRÖSSE / *GOTHIC GRANDEUR*

Als Bautyp ist St. Marien eine Basilika: Das Mittelschiff ragt zwischen den beiden Seitenschiffen heraus. So monumental und solide die Kirche scheint, sie bedarf der stützenden Strebbögen, um die Lasten ihres Mauerwerks aufzufangen und abzuleiten. Demselben Zweck dienen die eisernen Streben im Inneren, deren Einbau 1948 den Einsturz der teilzerstörten Kirche verhinderte.

In terms of its architectural form, St. Mary's is a basilica, with a high central nave flanked by two lower aisles. Though this church appears monumentally solid, it requires the support of buttresses, externally, and of iron braces, internally, to bear the load of the brick walls. The braces were added in 1948 to prevent the collapse of the church following bomb damage.

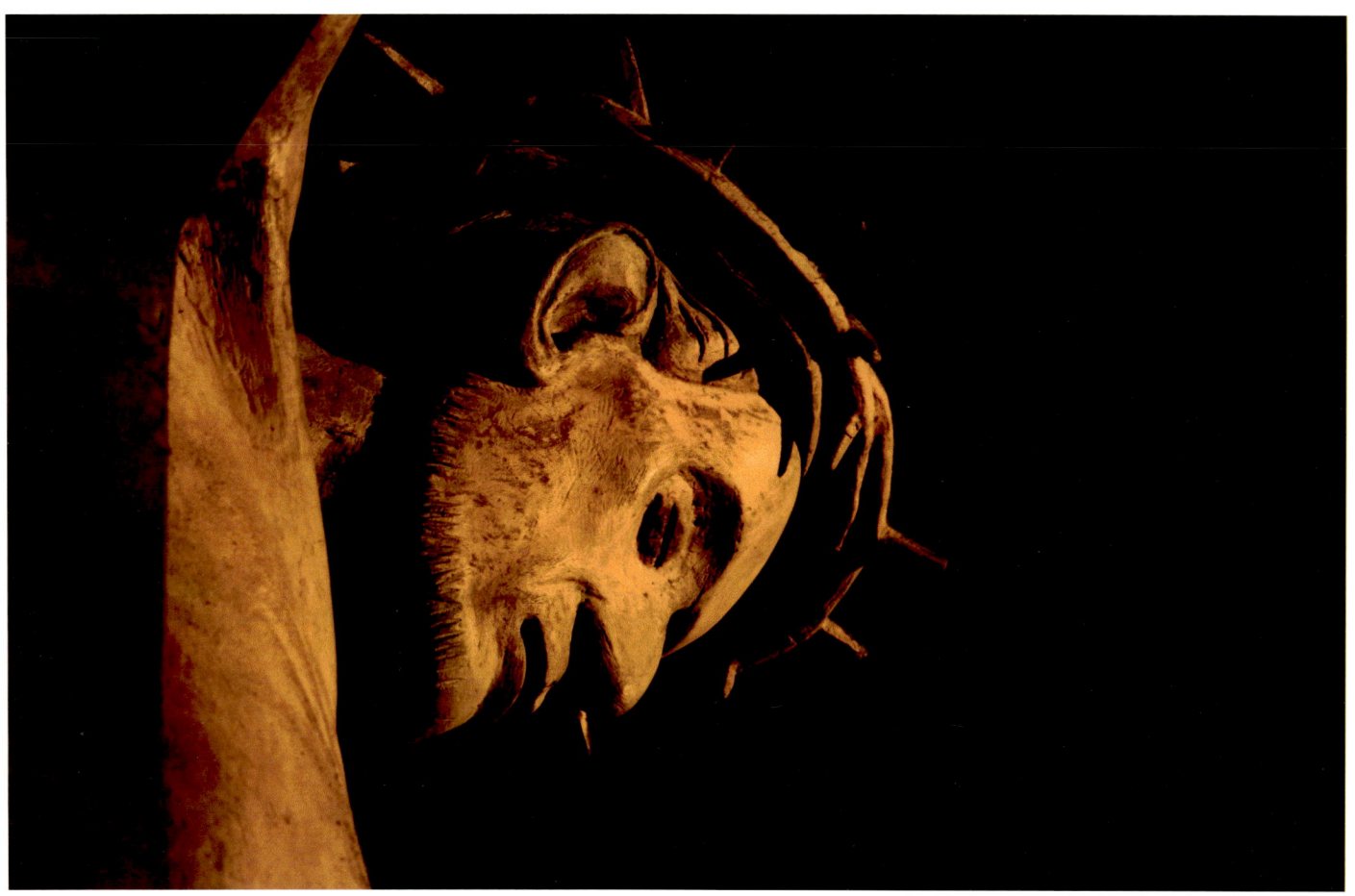

WARMES FARBSPIEL / *A WARM PLAY OF COLOUR*

1942 verbrannte die über Jahrhunderte gewachsene Ausstattung von St. Marien. Unter den weiß gekalkten Wänden traten alte warmtonige Malereien hervor. Der beschädigte barocke Fredenhagen-Altar wurde Ende der 1950er Jahre durch einen schlichten Altartisch ersetzt, über dem das von Gerhard Marcks gestaltete Kruzifix hängt. Wenige Wandmalereien, Leuchter und Epitaphien zeugen noch von der einstigen Fülle.

In 1942, the furnishings and décor of St. Mary's, which had gradually filled the church over centuries, were destroyed by fire. From behind the whitewashed walls emerged numerous paintings in warm hues. The bomb-damaged Baroque altarpiece by Thomas Quellinus (named the Fredenhagen Altar after its donor) was replaced in 1959 by a simple limestone altar and a bronze crucifix by Gerhard Marcks. The few surviving murals, candle holders and epitaphs serve as a reminder of this once-abundant interior.

TURMVERSAMMLUNG
A CONGREGATION OF SPIRES

St. Marien und das Rathaus stehen architektonisch und repräsentativ in enger Beziehung. Die Bürgermeister hatten ihr eigenes Gestühl in der Kirche, wichtiger Besuch wurde im Rathaus empfangen und durch St. Marien geführt. Kupferdächer und Backstein schaffen eine optische Verwandtschaft – und die kreisrunden Windlöcher in der hohen Schildwand bilden Gucklöcher.

St. Mary's and the neighbouring Rathaus (town hall) are closely related, both in terms of architecture and their roles in the life of Lübeck. The burgomasters of this prosperous city had their own pews in the church, and distinguished visitors were first received in the Rathaus, then given a tour of St. Mary's. The copper spires and red brick optically convey this relationship, as do the rounded holes in the market-facing wall; though designed to increase wind resistance, they offer peeks of the church from the town hall.

ST. MARIEN UND RATHAUS

ARCHITEKTUR-PUZZLE
AN ARCHITECTURAL PUZZLE

Das Rathaus, Sitz von Bürgermeister, Senat und Bürgerschaft, steht in Lübeck schlicht und einfach am Markt – und von dort aus sind die verschiedenen Bauteile vom 13. bis zum 16. Jahrhundert deutlich zu erkennen: die Schildwand aus dem 13. Jahrhundert, die drei Häuser zusammenfasste, rechts von ihr das Lange Haus (um 1300) und das Neue Gemach (1442–44), schließlich in Hellgrau die Renaissancelaube (1570–72). Aus dieser Zeit stammt ursprünglich auch die 1893/94 erneuerte Treppe.

Lübeck's Rathaus, seat of the city's mayor, senate, and legislative assembly, is strategically located overlooking the main market square. The building itself is an ensemble of various parts added between the 13th and 16th centuries, starting with the protective wall that connects three different buildings; the Long House (ca. 1300), which contained assembly and banquet halls, the New Chambers (1442–44), and the Renaissance Summerhouse (1570–72) which served as a courtroom. The Renaissance staircase was renovated in 1893–94.

RESPEKT, RESPEKT / *WITH ALL DUE RESPECT*

Es ist der dunkle Glanz des letzten Kaiserreichs, der sich in der Eingangshalle des Rathauses erhalten hat. Sie erhielt ihre Gestalt am Ende des 19. Jahrhunderts, als Senatoren und die Mitglieder der Bürgerschaft noch Zigarre statt Zigarette rauchten – der eigens dafür installierte Halter ist heute ein funktionsloses Kuriosum. Die Renaissancetür zum Audienzsaal wird umrahmt von älteren Relikten, darunter die Allegorien der Gerechtigkeit und der Weisheit.

The entrance hall to the Rathaus exudes a dark lustre representative of Germany's final monarchy. This space was decorated in the late 19th century, when senators and assemblymen smoked cigars rather than cigarettes. The specially designed cigar holder has been retained. No longer in use, it is a mere curiosity. The Renaissance door leading to the visitors' reception room is bordered by antique artefacts, including allegorical statues representing justice and wisdom.

RATHAUS 27

TREPPE MIT GESCHICHTE(N) / *A STORIED STAIRWAY*

Zwischen den dunkel glasierten Backsteinen leuchten die Farben im Treppenhaus besonders bunt. Drei große Wandgemälde des wilhelminischen Historienmalers Max Koch erzählen von der frühen Geschichte Lübecks. Im Oberlicht wacht das Lübecker Wappentier, der doppelköpfige Adler.

Amid the dark, glazed clinker, the colours of the stairway appear particularly vivid. Three large murals by the Wilhelmine historical painter Max Koch depict scenes from the early history of Lübeck. From the roof skylight, the double-headed eagle, the city's heraldic totem, keeps watch.

LÜBECK EMPFÄNGT / *LÜBECK'S FINEST ROOM*

Der Audienzsaal, ausgestattet um 1750, ist die gute Stube der Stadt, geöffnet nur für besondere Anlässe. Zwischen verspieltem Rokoko-Putz geben die allegorischen Gemälde von Stefano Torelli weise Ratschläge. Obwohl der Audienzsaal direkt an der geschäftigen Breiten Straße liegt, herrscht hier Stille.

The Audienzsaal or reception room was lavishly decorated around 1750 and is opened only on special occasions. Framed by playful Rococo stucco, the paintings by Stefano Torelli offer visitors nuggets of wisdom in allegorical form. Even though the Audienzsaal faces the busy Breite Strasse, it is a place of perfect stillness.

RATHAUS / AUDIENZSAAL

HERREN VON GESTERN / *GREAT MEN OF OLD*

Porträts von vielen Bürgermeistern schmücken die langen Gänge des Rathauses. Die ältesten Gemälde stammen aus dem 16. Jahrhundert; eine Bürgermeisterin fehlt noch. „Gebt dem Kaiser, was des Kaisers ist, und Gott, was Gottes ist": Die Tür unter dem Bibelspruch und Gemälde zum Zinsgroschen führte früher zur Kämmerei, der städtischen Finanzverwaltung.

Portraits of many former mayors adorn the long corridors of the Rathaus. The oldest of these dates from the sixteenth century. To date, all of Lübeck's mayors have been men. "Render unto Caesar the things that are Caesar's, and unto God the things that are God's": the door beneath the Bible verse in Latin and the painting depicting Jesus with the tribute coin used to lead to the city treasury.

DIE BÜRGERSCHAFT TAGT

Auch der Bürgerschaftssaal stammt vom Ende des 19. Jahrhunderts – hier wird die große und die kleine Politik der Hansestadt gemacht, geleitet von Stadtpräsidentin oder Stadtpräsident. Unter der Decke prangen bis heute die Wappen der Senatoren aus der Umbauzeit, auch das von Senator Mann, dem Vater von Heinrich und Thomas Mann.

THE ASSEMBLY SITS

The Assembly Hall was also decorated in the late nineteenth century. This is where the policies – great and small – of the city are forged, under the leadership of the mayor. The area beneath the roof is still decorated with the coats of arms of the senators from the period of reconstruction, among them Senator Mann, father of the writers Heinrich and Thomas Mann.

EINLADUNG ZUM BUMMELN / *AN INVITATION TO DAWDLE*

Gleich am Rathaus beginnt die lebendige Hüxstraße. Schon um 1900 eine der wichtigen Einkaufsstraßen der Stadt, ist sie heute Lübecks erste Adresse, wenn es um vielfältige inhabergeführte Läden und abwechslungsreiche Gastronomie in schönen Häusern geht. Am Sonnabend werden die Autos ausgesperrt – sie würden stören beim Bummeln.

The lively shopping street, Hüxstrasse, begins at the Rathaus. As early as 1900, this became one of the most important commercial locations in the city, and to this day, it is Lübeck's premier address for diverse owner-run shops and restaurants in some of the city's prettiest townhouses. On Saturdays, cars are banished from Hüxstrasse, so as not to disturb shoppers and diners.

VIEL ZU GUCKEN / *PLENTY TO SEE*

Schickes? Antikes? Lesenswertes? Nützliches? Alles im Angebot. Während sich für andere Einkaufsstraßen der Lübecker Innenstadt noch kein Rezept gegen zunehmende Leerstände gefunden hat, bleibt in der Hüxstraße kein Schaufenster länger ohne Auslage.

Whether you're looking for a cool shirt, an antique clock, a book to read, or a tool for home or garden, you're sure to find it on Hüxstrasse. While other parts of Lübeck's centre have rows of empty premises, every display window on this street is chock full of wares.

PLATZ ZUM VERWEILEN / *A PLACE TO LINGER*

Draußen sitzen bei Café oder Cocktail, Pasta oder Pizza – vor zehn Jahren noch kaum denkbar: die Eroberung der Straße durch die Gastronomie und ihre Gäste. In der benachbarten Fleischhauerstraße müssen für diesen Zweck auch Autos auf ihren vermeintlich angestammten Platz verzichten.

Just ten years ago, al fresco dining was unheard of in Lübeck. Today, the streets have been conquered by cafés, bars, and restaurants. Neighbouring Fleischhauerstrasse has even been fully pedestrianised to allow for undisturbed sipping of cocktails and enjoyment of pizza and pasta.

GOLDENES LICHT / *GOLDEN LIGHT*

Entweder sind Straßen in der Altstadt lang, weil sie sich als „Rippenstraßen" von der Achse bis zum Wasser hinabziehen. Oder sie sind als Querstraße nur kurz, verbinden zwei Rippenstraßen und teilen so einen langgezogenen Baublock. Die Häuser sind immer hübsch eingereiht – das gab die Bauordnung des 13. Jahrhunderts vor, die bis ins Kaiserreich Gesetzeskraft hatte.

The streets in Lübeck's Altstadt are either long because they act as ribs connecting the central axes to the river, or short cross streets connecting the ribs and forming rectangular blocks. The houses are arranged in attractive and orderly rows, in accordance with a building code that was in force from the 13th right up to the late 19th century.

42   RIPPEN- UND QUERSTRASSEN

44 FLEISCHHAUERSTRASSE / GROSSE BURGSTRASSE

DIE STRASSE WIRD ZUR BÜHNE
THE STREET TAKES CENTRE STAGE

Sitzen, sehen und gesehen werden: Die Fleischhauerstraße hat sich innerhalb kurzer Zeit zu einer bunten Meile entwickelt – mehr Stühle und Tische, weniger Parkplätze ist das einfache Erfolgsrezept. Kneipen und eine junge Gastronomie erwecken die historische Straße neu. Auch die Straßenbühne vor dem „Tonfink" in der Großen Burgstraße gibt es noch nicht lange. Sie ist ein weiteres Zeichen für einen menschenfreundlichen Wandel an einer zu viel befahrenen Altstadtstraße.

Fleischhauerstrasse has lately become one of Lübeck's hotspots, the place to sit, see and be seen. The magic formula: more chairs and tables, and fewer parked cars. Pubs and new restaurants that attract a younger crowd are breathing fresh life into this historic street. The recently erected stage outside the Tonfink Kulturcafé in Grosse Burgstrasse is a further sign that the once-congested Altstadt is becoming a more welcoming and leisurely place.

FREIRAUM MIT KANTEN

Lübeck kann auch rau sein, kantig und derb – und ganz bunt auf Backstein. Spielplätze gibt es in der Altstadt höchstens dort, wo alte Architektur gewichen ist, durch Zerstörung oder Abriss. Junge Leute haben in den letzten Jahren die hafennahe Clemensstraße erobert – in den hundert Jahren zuvor war sie der Ort behördlich zugelassener Prostitution.

GRITTY PLAYGROUND

Lübeck is not all pretty shopfronts and majestic churches. It also has plenty of rough edges, though the ubiquitous brick lends a splash of colour to even the dingiest dives. The old city doesn't have many playgrounds – except where bomb damage or demolition opened gaps in the original architectural fabric. In recent years, young people have adopted Clemensstrasse, close to a century Lübeck's official red-light district, as their urban playground.

VOM HANDWERK ZUM KUNSTWERK / *FROM CRAFT TO ART*

Viele Straßennamen in der Altstadt verraten, welche Berufsgruppen im Mittelalter dort ansässig waren. In der hafennahen Böttcherstraße waren die Fassmacher tätig, deren Behältnisse für wasserdichte Transporte dienten. Heute arbeitet hier die Bildhauerin Bettina Thierig. Aus Stein, Holz und Metall entstehen ihre Skulpturen, stumm, aber vielfältig sprechend als neue Bewohnerschaft einer alten Gasse.

Many of the street names in Lübeck's Altstadt are named after the group of craftsmen who lived and worked there during the Middle Ages. Böttcherstrasse, which is situated close to the port, was home to the city's guild of coopers, who made a variety of containers for transporting liquid goods. Today, the artist Bettina Thierig works here, creating sculptures from stone, wood, and metal.

48   ATELIER BETTINA THIERIG

RETTENDE HÄNDE / *PRESERVING HANDS*

Ein Teil der Lübecker Altstadt ist seit 1987 Weltkulturerbe, und dazu gehören natürlich die Kirchen. Um ihren Erhalt kümmern sich Handwerker, die ebenfalls „Weltkulturgut" sind: 2020 nahm die UNESCO die seit dem Mittelalter bestehenden europäischen Kirchenbauhütten in ihr Verzeichnis des immateriellen Kulturerbes der Menschheit auf. Hat die Kirchenbauhütte einen Turm saniert, folgt gleich der nächste. Denn Umwelteinflüsse setzen den Kirchen unablässig zu.

Part of Lübeck's Altstadt was declared a UNESCO World Heritage site in 1987, and naturally, that includes first and foremost its churches. The skilled craftsmen responsible for their conservation are also part of the world's cultural patrimony, as Europe's church masons' guilds, which have existed since the Middle Ages, have been recognized by UNESCO since 2020 as part of the world's intangible cultural heritage. Once Lübeck's church masons have finished refurbishing one church steeple, the next awaits them – because the churches are subject to unrelenting environmental impacts.

MIT BACKSTEIN ZUM HIMMEL / *TOWERING BRICK*

Die letzte Eiszeit hat zwar jede Menge Findlinge nach Norddeutschland gebracht, aber große Haussteine mussten von weither geholt werden. Im 12. Jahrhundert brachten Handwerker aus der Lombardei die Kunst des Backsteinbaus in den Norden. Zunächst waren es Kirchen und Klöster, die mit dem neuen Material errichtet wurden. St. Marien strahlte als Bauwerk weit aus und diente als Vorbild für rund siebzig Kirchen im Ostseeraum.

The glaciers of the last Ice Age carried plenty of erratic boulders to Northern Germany, but large cut masonry stone had to be brought from further afield. In the twelfth century, craftsmen from Lombardy brought the art of brickmaking to the North. Soon, this new material was being used to build churches and monasteries. St. Mary's in Lübeck gained renown and served as a model for around seventy other churches in the Baltic region.

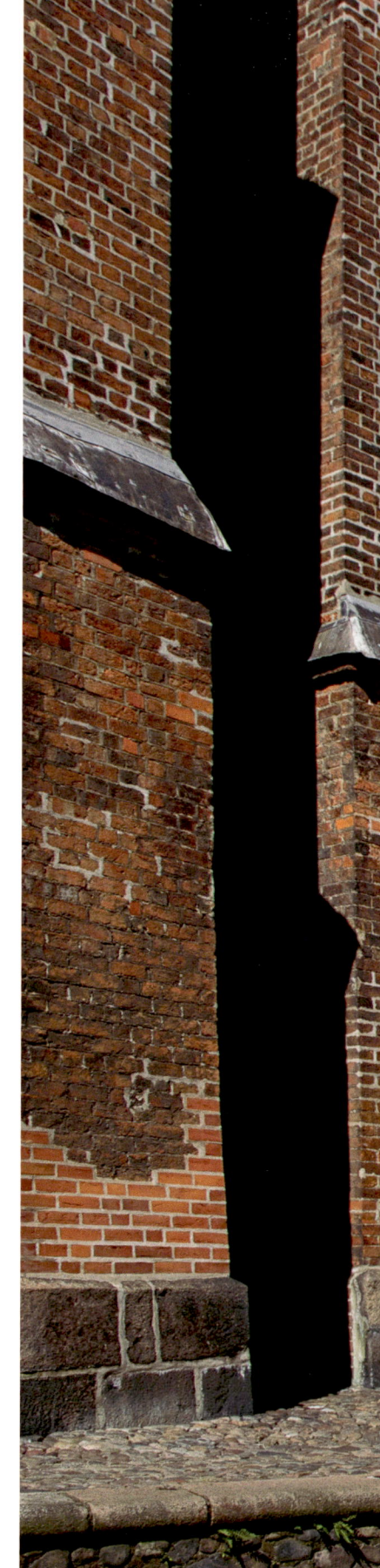

MAUER-WERKE / *BRICK-WORK*

Nicht jeder Backstein hält ewig – das ist an vielen Bauwerken zu erkennen. Kundige Augen können an geflickten Mauern die jahrhundertelange Baugeschichte ablesen wie an der hohen Stützmauer in der Kleinen Altefähre beim Burgkloster (links) oder am gotischen Chor von Jakobi und den Pastorenhäusern (rechts).

Not every clinker brick stands the test of time, as evidenced by the patches on many of Lübeck's older brick structures. A trained eye will quickly spot where over the centuries walls have been repaired. Examples include the high supporting wall that runs along Kleine Altefähre near the Burgkloster friary (left), the Gothic choir in St. James' Church (St. Jakobi), and the ministers' homes (right).

ERSTES HOSPITAL AM PLATZ
FIRST HOME FOR THE ELDERLY

Seit acht Jahrhunderten steht das Heiligen-Geist-Hospital mit seiner von Türmchen gezierten Fassade am Koberg. Bis heute ist es ein Seniorenheim, entstanden im 13. Jahrhundert als mildtätige Stiftung. Hinter der Fassade steckt eine Kirche, der Wohntrakt liegt im rückseitigen Bereich. Der Koberg vor dem Hospital ist ein großer Platz, dessen Weite auch manchen in Lübeck Wohnenden irritiert. Dafür bietet er Raum für temporäre Projekt wie das Urban Gardening auf dem Foto links.

The Hospice of the Holy Spirit, with its four minaret-like spires and ornate façade, has stood at Koberg square for eight hundred years. Founded in the 13th century as a charity, to this day it functions as a home for the aged infirm. Behind the façade stands a church, with the living quarters in the rear. Koberg square is uncharacteristically expansive for Lübeck, too much so for some residents' taste. It offers ample space for temporary projects such as the urban gardens pictured left.

HEILIGEN-GEIST-HOSPITAL

KLASSIZISTISCHE KLARHEIT
CLASSICAL CLARITY

Es dauerte lange, bis die Reformierte Gemeinde innerhalb der Stadt ihre eigene Kirche bauen durfte. Denn die strenge lutherische Geistlichkeit erlaubte dies ebenso wenig wie den Bau einer Synagoge. Das Bilderverbot des reformierten Glaubens lässt die monumentale Saalkirche kühl erscheinen, die großen Fenster aber sorgen für ein warmes Licht auf Gestühl und Orgel.

It took a long time before the Calvinist congregation in the city was permitted to build its own church. Lübeck's strict Lutheran clergy opposed this as vehemently as they opposed the construction of a synagogue. The Reformed faith does not permit sacred imagery, and as a result, the monumental single-nave church appears cool and austere. Thankfully, the large windows flood the room with sunlight and shine a warm light on the pews and organ.

HISTORISCHE WOHNKULTUR / *HISTORICAL HOME DECOR*

Im 1915 eröffneten St. Annen-Museum haben sich die historischen Zeugnisse von Kunst, Leben und Arbeiten in Lübeck vom Mittelalter bis in das 19. Jahrhundert versammelt. Unterkunft fanden hier nach der Gründung des Museums auch Raumausstattungen wie die große Diele. Sie stammt aus einem Haus in der Glockengießerstraße. Eigens für die hohen und tiefen Dielen entwickelte sich der voluminöse „Schapp" (Schrank) als typisches Lübecker Möbel.

Founded in 1915, St. Anne's Museum houses a collection comprising historical artefacts that reflect the artistic, professional, and domestic life of Lübeck from the Middle Ages to the 19th century. The museum also includes several examples of furnished home interiors, such as the big hall (pictured left), taken from a house on Glockengießerstrasse. The hefty Schapp wardrobe was a piece of furniture specially designed in Lübeck for such large hallways.

ST. ANNEN-MUSEUM

SCHÖNSTES WOHNEN / *LIVING IN STYLE*

Gerettet: Beinahe wäre 1921 aus dem Behnhaus, einem der schönsten und großzügigsten Bürgerhäuser, eine nüchterne Bankfiliale geworden. Heute vereint es zusammen mit dem benachbarten Drägerhaus in idealer Weise die original erhaltenen Räume und präsentiert historisches Wohnen sowie bildende Kunst. Zur Sammlung gehören Werke von Caspar David Friedrich, Johann Friedrich Overbeck, Edvard Munch und Max Liebermann.

The Behn House, one of Lübeck's most sumptuous townhouses, was nearly converted to a bank branch in 1921. Luckily it was saved from that sober fate. Alongside the neighbouring Dräger House, the perfectly maintained interiors and artwork reflect bourgeois life in Lübeck during the city's halcyon days. The art collection includes works by Caspar David Friedrich, Johann Friedrich Overbeck, Edvard Munch, and Max Liebermann.

ANDERS WOHNEN
ALTERNATIVE LIVING

Kein Haus ist in der Lübecker Altstadt wie das andere. Und jedes Haus hat seine Geschichte. So wie das Berkentienhaus, in dem vom 17. Jahrhundert bis 1995 eine Glaserei-Werkstatt ansässig war. Von ihr findet man heute noch viele Spuren im Haus. Eine nicht nur finanzielle Herausforderung ist es, in solchen Häusern heutigen Ansprüchen beim Wohnen und den Vorgaben des Denkmalschutzes zugleich gerecht zu werden.

No house in Lübeck's Altstadt is quite like the other – each has its unique history, the Berkentien House, for example, which was home to a glass-making studio from the 17th century right up until 1995. Traces of that craft can be found throughout the house. It is a formidable challenge, and not just a question of cost, to reconcile the strict rules around the development of historical buildings with the requirements of a modern and liveable home.

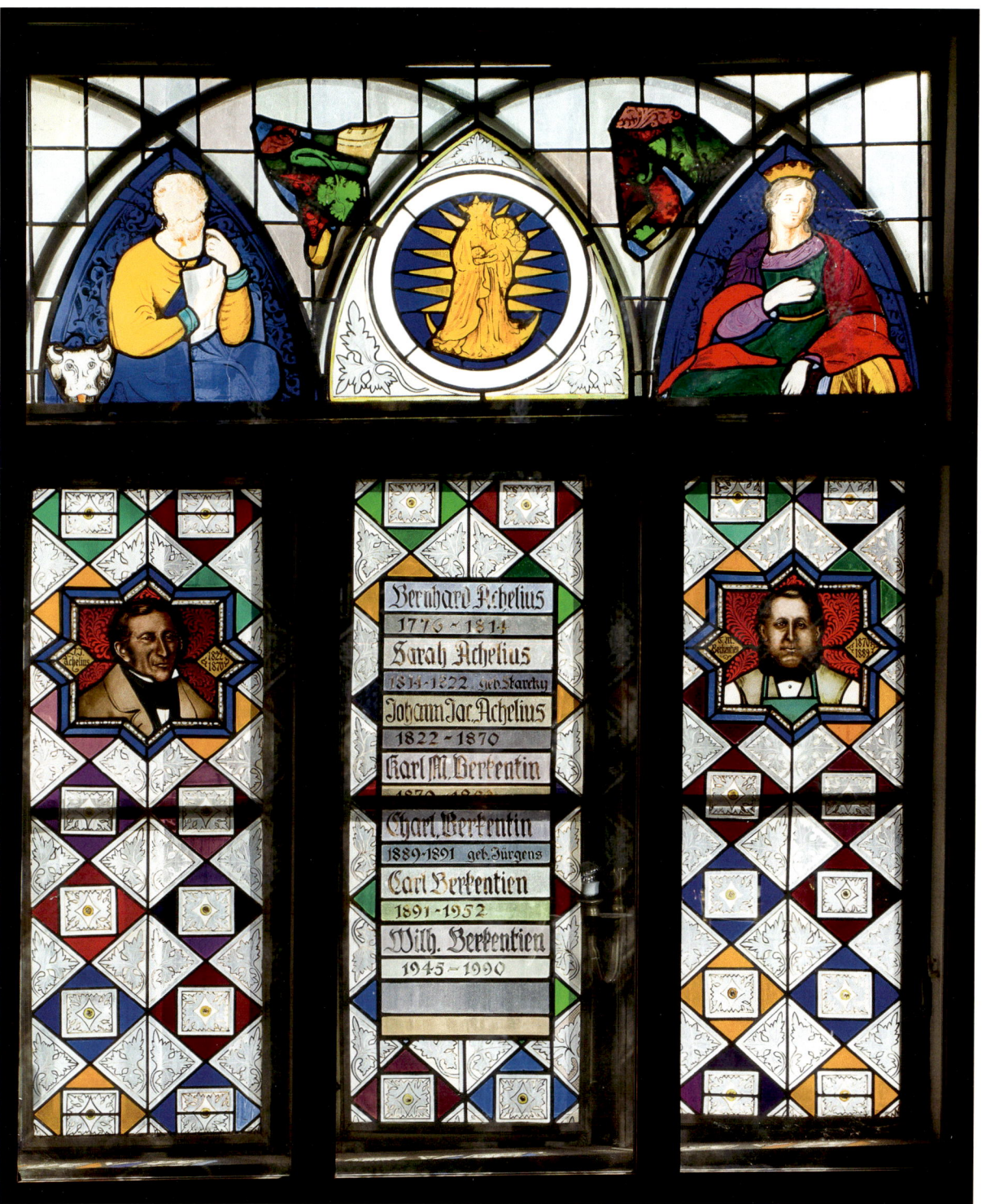

BERKENTIENHAUS

66 GLASMANUFAKTUR ROTTER

HANDWERKS-KUNST / *FINE CRAFTSMANSHIP*

Mit ausgefeilter Technik bringen Glasschleifer der Glasmanufaktur Rotter schillernd leuchtende Farben in geometrischen Formen hervor. Ursprünglich kam der Betrieb 1945 aus Stettin nach Lübeck. Die Erfahrung von Migration gab Anlass für den Entwurf einer besonderen Vase in jüngster Zeit: Sie zeigt kulturelle Vielfalt und einen Auszug aus der Allgemeinen Erklärung der Menschenrechte der Vereinten Nationen.

Applying finely honed techniques, the glass cutters at Rotter Glass draw out geometric forms in bright shimmering colours. The company was originally founded in Stettin (modern-day Szczecin in Poland) but was relocated to Lübeck in 1945. The experience of forced migration inspired the design of a very special vase: it represents cultural diversity and includes an excerpt from the UN Universal Declaration of Human Rights.

LECKERE KUNSTWERKE / *TASTY WORKS OF ART*

So wenig wie ohne Backstein, so wenig kann man sich Lübeck ohne Marzipan vorstellen. Das ist vor allem dem Konditor Johann Georg Niederegger zu verdanken, der Marzipan aus Lübeck im 19. Jahrhundert zum Exportschlager machte. Die Herstellung der leckeren Süßigkeit, ihre Geschichte und Verarbeitung, wird im Schauraum über dem Café Niederegger in der Breiten Straße erzählt.

Marzipan is an integral to Lübeck as red brick, thanks to the confectioner Johann Georg Niederegger, who made Lübeck Marzipan world famous in the 19th century. The story of this delicious sweet – its history and the process of manufacturing – is told in the showroom above Café Niederegger on Breite Strasse.

NIEDEREGGER MARZIPANSALON

70 SCHIFFERGESELLSCHAFT

TAFELN IN TRADITION / *BOARDS STEEPED IN TRADITION*

„Allen zu gefallen ist unmöglich", liest man außen am Eingang – aber Lübecks historische Schiffergesellschaft gefällt allen. Der Bau aus dem 16. Jahrhundert war ursprünglich das Versammlungshaus der Schiffer. Seit bald zweihundert Jahren ist es aber auch eine Gaststätte, in der Schiffsmodelle, Gemälde und Schnitzereien von der Lübecker Seefahrt erzählen.

The words "It's impossible to please everyone" are written above the entrance – although Lübeck's historical Skippers' Society may be the exception to that rule. The building dates from the 16th century and was originally the assembly hall of the city's sea captains. For close to two hundred years, it has served as a restaurant, in which model ships, maritime paintings and sculptures tell the story of Lübeck's seafaring tradition.

SCHWIMMENDES MUSEUM / *A FLOATING MUSEUM*

1911 lief sie in Hamburg vom Stapel. 39-mal umrundete sie Kap Horn. Die *Passat* brachte Salpeter und später Getreide von Südamerika nach Deutschland. Als frachtfahrendes Schulschiff ging sie 1952 noch auf große Fahrt – bis 1957 ihr Schwesterschiff im Atlantik sank. Heute ist sie Denkmal und Museum der Segelschifffahrt.

The Passat was launched in Hamburg in 1911. Thirty-nine times she rounded Cape Horn, carrying first saltpetre and later grain from South America to Germany. By 1952 she was still in service – as a training vessel for freight shipping. After her sister ship sank in the Atlantic, she was finally retired. Today, the Passat houses the Museum of Sailing and serves as a historical monument in her own right.

AUF ANS NEUE UFER / *ON THE WATERFRONT*

Die *Passat* hat viele Nachbarn – unzählige Segelboote liegen im Passathafen auf dem Priwall in Travemünde, der Halbinsel östlich der Travemündung. Die Segler sind hier aber nicht mehr unter sich – mit der Neubebauung entlang des Ufers lässt sich hier nun Urlaub ohne Wasser unter dem Kiel machen. Die *Passat* stört das nicht.

The four-master sailing ship Passat is in good company – countless sailboats are moored in the Passathafen Marina on the Priwall Peninsula in Travemünde, east of the Trave River estuary. But sailing enthusiasts are no longer alone – new developments along the shore have also attracted holidaymakers who prefer to keep their feet on solid ground.

FERNWEH RICHTUNG NORDEN / *NORTHBOUND*

Jeden Tag fahren die „großen Pötte" in den Hafen von Travemünde ein, machen an einem der Anleger des Skandinavienkais fest und legen nach wenigen Stunden wieder ab. Mit den kombinierten Fracht- und Passagierschiffen ist Travemünde größter deutscher Fährhafen mit Routen nach Schweden, Finnland und ins Baltikum.

Every day, large vessels enter the Port of Travemünde, dock at the Skandinavienkai and depart within a few hours. With facilities for both cargo and passenger ships, Travemünde is Germany's largest ferry port with routes to Sweden, Finland, and the Baltic states.

MEER INSPIRIERT / *INSPIRED BY THE SEA*

Das Segeln gehört seit Kaisers Zeiten zu Travemünde. Aus den Regatten, die sich Wilhelm II. mit hanseatischen Kaufleuten lieferte, entwickelte sich die Travemünder Woche. Für die in Travemünde lebende und arbeitende Malerin Frauke Klatt dagegen liefern Boote, Wellen, Himmel und Wolken unerschöpfliche Inspiration für ihre „Bilder vom Segeln".

Sailing has been at the heart of Travemünde since the days of the Kaiser. The Travemünde Week (Travemünder Woche), an annual sailing event, gained popularity after Wilhelm II competed against Hanseatic merchants and won. Boats, waves, clouds, and the sky provide Frauke Klatt, an artist who lives and works in Travemünde, with an endless source of inspiration for her 'paintings of sailing'.

ATELIER FRAUKE KLATT

ES IST ETWAS IM GANG / *TUCKED AWAY*

Sie sind eine Lübecker Spezialität – die Wohngänge. Rund hundert von einst zweihundert gibt es noch heute, bebaut mit kleinen oder noch kleineren „Buden", die im Mittelalter mehr Wohnraum in der ummauerten Altstadt schufen. Heute sind die ehemals einfachen Quartiere meist top saniert und beliebt bei kleinen Haushalten.

WEBERSTRASSE / AN DER MAUER

LÜBECK BLÜHT / *LÜBECK IN BLOOM*

An manchen Stellen verschwinden Mauern, Türen und Fußwege hinter und unter prächtigen Rosenstöcken. Finden kann man sie in den Seiten- und Querstraßen, wo die Passierenden ohne Gefahr auf das Kopfsteinpflaster ausweichen können. Schon im 14. Jahrhundert gab es die Straße Rosengarten – an ihr lag der Garten des Frauenklosters St. Johannis.

In some places, walls, doorways, and footpaths disappear behind and under magnificent rose bushes, usually in the side and cross streets. Pedestrians can avoid their thorns by walking on the cobblestones. Rosengarten is a street laid out in the 14th century, and where the garden of St. John's Convent used to be – hence its name.

AM STRAND IN TRAVEMÜNDE

BADEN, BEWEGEN, BESINNEN / *FOR BODY AND SOUL*

„Und dann die See, sie haben die Ostsee dort oben! …" – so liest man in Thomas Manns *Tonio Kröger*. Keine Frage: Die Meeresnähe ist einer der großen Vorzüge von Lübeck. Und der Schriftsteller beschreibt in den *Buddenbrooks* auch die wechselnden Stimmungen am Meer, wo es nie langweilig ist, wo man auf das Wasser schaut oder in sich hinein.

"And then the sea – they have the Baltic Sea up there!…" Thomas Mann's Tonio Kröger exclaims. There's no question about it: Lübeck's proximity to the sea is one of its great draws. And in Buddenbrooks, Mann describes the changing moods of the sea, where it's never dull, where one can gaze out over the water and lose oneself in contemplation.

Secluded residential lanes, alleyways and courtyards are a special feature of Lübeck. Once they numbered two hundred, today there are about a hundred of them filled with cottages and tiny houses built in the Middle Ages to create additional living space within the walls of the old city. Most of the once rudimentary courtyard homes have been tastefully refurbished and are highly prized by couples and small families.

KLEIN, ABER GRÜN / *SMALL AND LUSH*

Der Rosengang – auf dem Foto links –, wie dürfte es anders sein, ziert sich mit Rosen. So klein die Gangbuden sind, so wichtig ist der Außenplatz, vorzüglich mit einer Bank, die zur Lektüre unter freiem Himmel oder zum Plausch mit den Nachbarn einlädt. Wenn nur nicht die manchmal allzu vielen neugierigen Touristen stören würden ...

Covered in roses, the Rosengang – the walkway pictured on the left – certainly lives up to its name. Since the cottages are so small, the outdoor spaces are very important. There's usually a bench or two, where residents can pass time outside, reading or chatting with their neighbours. If only the many curious tourists weren't sometimes such a nuisance...

RUHE FÜR DEN RUHESTAND

Nicht grüner, aber größer sind die Stiftungshöfe, in denen früher anständige Frauen, unverheiratet oder verwitwet, ihren Lebensabend verbringen konnten. Bis heute dienen sie demselben Zweck, noch immer von Stiftungen getragen, die einst von Kaufleuten zur Sicherung ihres Seelenheils errichtet wurden.

A PEACEFUL RETIREMENT

The courtyards belonging to charitable foundations (Stiftungshöfe) are similarly green but considerably larger. They provided housing to respectable spinsters or widows, who were allowed to live out their twilight years there. To this day, they still serve the same purpose, run by the foundations originally established by wealthy merchants in the hope of securing heavenly salvation through good works.

KRAFTSTOFF KUNST / *CULTURAL FILLING STATION*

Ein Denkmal der Automobilität sind die Überreste der Tankstelle aus den 1930er Jahren unmittelbar neben dem Holstentor. Heute ist das Ensemble ein kreativer Ort für die freien Künste: eine Halle für Ausstellungen, Garagen als Ateliers, Freiflächen für Veranstaltungen. Hier lässt sich gesellig auftanken. Und auch die Bilder des Lübecker Künstlers Felix Karweick fühlen sich, präsentiert im Garten, sehr wohl.

A monument to early automobility: the remains of a large petrol station from the 1930s next to the Holsten Gate. Today, it serves as an arts centre with an exhibition hall, garages converted to studios, and a garden space overlooking the Trave that is used for events. This is the perfect place to socialise and recharge one's batteries – for example at an exhibition by the Lübeck-based painter Felix Karweick.

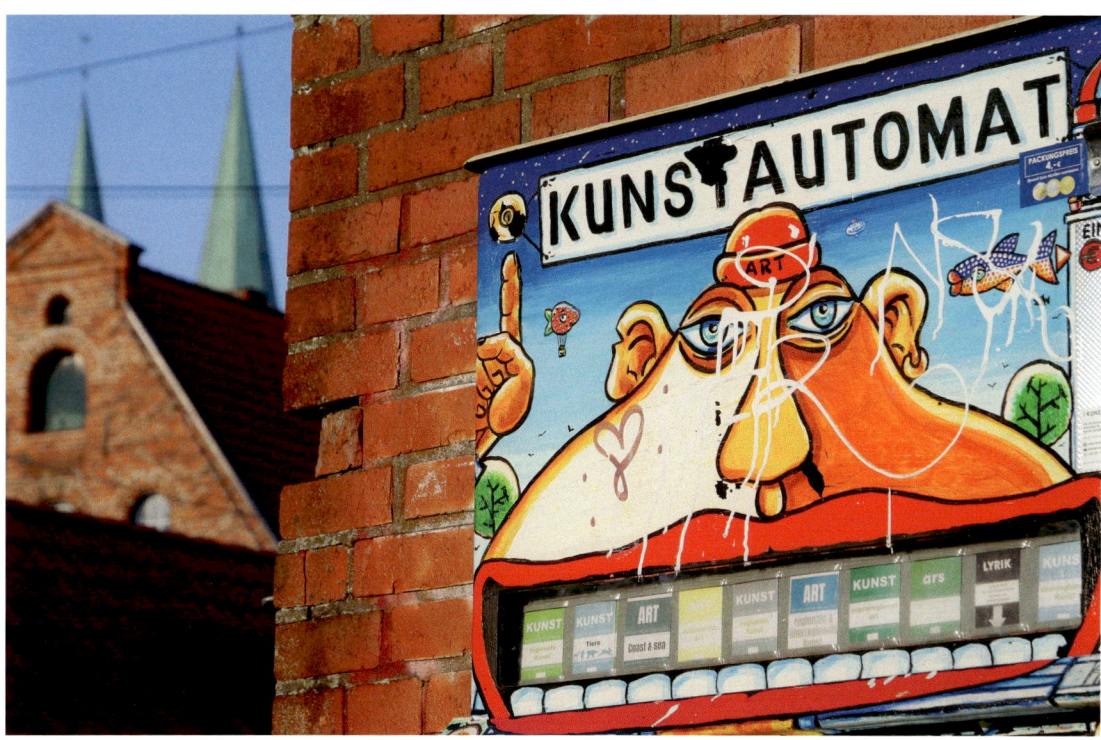

KUNSTTANKSTELLE 93

AM SONNENUFER
THE SUN SETS IN THE WEST

Wie in anderen Hafenstädten gewinnen auch in Lübeck alte Hafenflächen und -gebäude neue Bedeutung für den Aufenthalt im städtischen Raum. Den Museumshafen an der Untertrave gibt es schon lange, noch neu ist der Drehbrückenplatz, dessen Ränge am Wasser sich bei gutem Wetter schnell füllen – denn hier auf der Westseite der Altstadt lässt sich die Sonne bis in den Abend genießen.

For decades, the west side of the old town was one thing above all: a parking lot. As in other European cities, the rediscovery of the city harbour has created new areas for life on the water. And Lübeck is lucky that the old quays and the new swing bridge square are the best stage for the sunset.

LEBEN AM WASSER / *LIFE ON THE WATER*

Abendbrot im Abendrot, und nebenan hängt die Wäsche draußen – das geht an der Obertrave. Das Domviertel gehört zu den ruhigsten Quartieren der Altstadt, abgesehen vom regen Wasserverkehr an sonnigen Tagen. Die Elektroboote, mit denen sich sehr entschleunigt die Altstadtinsel umrunden lässt, sind aber ganz still.

Dinner al fresco in the late afternoon sun and laundry hanging out to dry – those are still common sights on the Upper Trave. The area around the cathedral is one of the quietest in the Altstadt, apart from the busy traffic on the water when the weather is good. Fortunately, the boats that offer sightseeing tours around the Altstadt island are electric and therefore very quiet.

TAUCHEN UNTER TÜRMEN / *BATHING WITH THE CROWS*

Eine wirkliche Insel ist die Lübecker Altstadt erst seit dem Jahr 1900, als der Elbe-Lübeck-Kanal eröffnet wurde. Weil die Traveseite zwar idyllisch, aber zu stark befahren ist, darf man dort nicht baden. Das geht dafür auf der anderen Stadtseite am Krähenteich, wo die Altstadt schon seit über einhundert Jahren ihre eigene Badeanstalt hat.

Lübeck's Altstadt only became an island when the Elbe-Lübeck Canal opened in 1900. The Trave side is idyllic but very busy, so swimming is not permitted. It is possible to swim on the other side of the island, at Crows' Pond (Krähenteich), which has served as a natural swimming pool for over a century.

ÜBER DEN DÄCHERN VON LÜBECK
OVER THE ROOFS OF LÜBECK

Von der Brücke an der Possehlstraße bietet sich zu jeder Jahreszeit ein Postkartenblick auf die Häuser an der Obertrave und die sie überragenden Domtürme. Hier lässt sich alles Moderne ausblenden, sieht man vom regen Wasserverkehr aller Art ab. Nicht ausblenden lassen sich die Bauschäden an den 800 Jahre alten Domtürmen – die nächste Sanierung steht an.

At any time of year, the bridge on Possehlstrasse offers picture-postcard views of the houses on the Upper Trave and the cathedral spires towering behind them. It's the perfect place to escape modern life – as long as you ignore the constant bustle of river traffic. The state of disrepair of the 800-year-old cathedral spires is harder to ignore. Restoration work is urgently needed.

GOTISCHE GRÖSSE / *GOTHIC GRACE*

St. Katharinen hat als einstige Bettelordenskirche nur einen Dachreiter und keinen Turm. Doch ihr Kirchenschiff muss sich nicht verstellen – wie könnte es auch, ragt es doch mächtig und selbstbewusst über die Häuser der Glockengießerstraße empor. Den Franziskanern als Bauherren halfen die großzügigen Vermächtnisse vermögender Lübecker und Lübeckerinnen, für deren Seelenheil die Mönche Messen lasen.

As a church that was once belonged to a mendicant order, St. Catherine's has just one ridge turret and no steeple. But its imposing nave above the houses of Glockengiesserstrasse is impossible to miss. The generous bequests made by wealthy townspeople helped the Franciscans build it; in return, the monks said masses for their salvation.

ST. KATHARINEN

GEDENKT DER TOTEN / *REMEMBER THE DEAD*

Wer es sich leisten konnte, kaufte eine Grabstätte in einer der Kirchen; die Ärmeren mussten sich mit dem Grab auf einem umliegenden Kirchhof begnügen oder gar mit dem Armenfriedhof vor der Stadt. Das galt vom Mittelalter bis nach 1800. In St. Katharinen lässt sich die Vielfalt der bürgerlichen Begräbniskultur entdecken: vom gotischen Wandgemälde über die Grabplatten aus allen Jahrhunderten bis zu den barocken Kapellen und Epitaphien.

From the Middle Ages until well into the 19th century, those who could afford it bought a crypt in one of the churches; the poor had to make do with a grave in the churchyard or even one in the paupers' cemetery outside of the city. St. Catherine's gives visitors the opportunity to discover the funeral culture of the nobility and burghers over the centuries: from Gothic frescoes to grave slabs to Baroque chapels and epitaphs.

ANDENKEN AN ASSISI / *A NOD TO ASSISI*

Ein zweistöckiger Chor ist eine Besonderheit gotischer Franziskanerkirchen. Denn er erinnert an das Vorbild der Basilika San Francesco in Assisi, wo der Ordensgründer bestattet ist. Die große Reiterskulptur des Drachentöters St. Jürgen zeugt dagegen von der Bedeutung, die Lübeck als Kunstmetropole des Mittelalters für den Ostseeraum hatte: Die Skulptur ist ein Abguss von 1926, das Original steht in Stockholm.

A two-storey choir is a feature of Gothic Franciscan churches. It is reminiscent of the upper and lower levels of the Basilica of St. Francis in Assisi, where the founder of the order is buried. The large equestrian sculpture Saint George and the Dragon by Bernt Notke bears witness to the city's importance in the Baltic region as a centre for art in the Middle Ages. The sculpture is a replica cast in 1926; the wooden original is in Stockholm.

UNBEKANNTER UNTERGRUND / *UNDERGROUND VAULTS*

Viele historische Häuser der Lübecker Altstadt erheben sich auf historischen Kellern aus dem Mittelalter. Sie dienten als Lagerraum, aber auch als Verkaufs- oder Wohnkeller. Die Reformierte Kirche, ein mächtiger klassizistischer Bau von 1826, steht über den Kellern der drei Häuser, die für ihren Bau weichen mussten. Bis vor wenigen Jahren diente dieser klimatisch ideale Lagerraum dem traditionsreichen Weinhaus von Melle.

Many historic houses in Lübeck's old city were built on cellars dating back to the Middle Ages. They were used for storage but also as shops and dwellings. The Reformed Church, an imposing neo-classical building, was built in 1826 above the cellars of the three houses that had to make way for its construction. Until a few years ago, they provided ideal storage space for H.F. von Melle, one of Lübeck's oldest wine merchants.

GESCHÄNDET, ABER GERETTET / *SURVIVOR*

Wie fast alle Synagogen in Deutschland wurde auch in Lübeck das jüdische Gotteshaus in der St.-Annen-Straße 1938 geschändet und verwüstet. Das Gebäude blieb erhalten, weil es bereits kurz vor der Pogromnacht in den Besitz der Stadt übergegangen war. Bei der 2020 abgeschlossenen Sanierung kamen viele Elemente der ursprünglichen Ausstattung zum Vorschein. Über die Geschichte des Gotteshauses, das wieder im Besitz der jüdischen Gemeinde ist, informiert eine Dauerausstellung.

Like almost all synagogues in Germany, the Jewish house of worship in St. Annen Strasse in Lübeck was desecrated and vandalised in 1938. The building was preserved because it had already come into the city's possession shortly before the Kristallnacht pogroms. During its restoration, completed in 2020, many of its original fittings and furnishings were discovered. A permanent exhibition provides information on the history of the synagogue, which is once again owned by the Jewish community.

SYNAGOGE

PRACHT DES MITTELALTERS / *MEDIEVAL SPLENDOUR*

Hier herrscht jeden Tag großer Konvent der Heiligen: Das St. Annen-Museum versammelt die mittelalterlichen Altäre und Skulpturen aus der Zeit, als Lübeck Kunsthauptstadt für das nördliche Europa war. Einen schöneren und stimmigeren Platz als das spätgotische St.-Annen-Kloster, Anfang des 16. Jahrhunderts errichtet, kann es für sie nicht geben. Raumfluchten und Durchblicke öffnen immer wieder neue Perspektiven.

A great gathering of saints: St. Anne's Museum brings them together in medieval altars and sculptures from when Lübeck was the art capital of northern Europe. There could not be a more beautiful and more appropriate place for them than St. Anne's Monastery, a late Gothic structure built in the early 16th century. Long enfilades give visitors a glimpse of things to come.

GESCHICHTEN AM RANDE / *PICTURE BOOKS OF THE MIDDLE AGES*

Bilderbücher des Mittelalters: Im Zentrum der Altäre stehen die Lebensgeschichten der Heiligen. Drum herum aber nutzten die Künstler den Freiraum auch, um ihn mit alltäglichen Szenen zu füllen. Diese sind dramatisch, anrührend, humorvoll und kurios und erzählen als abwechslungsreiche Nebengeschichten vom einstigen Leben in Lübeck: von Kindheit, Haustieren, Mode, Essen und Trinken und anderem.

The altars of St. Anne's are dedicated to depicting the lives of the saints. The artists also included dramatic, touching, humorous, and intriguing scenes showing children, pets, fashion, food, and drink, giving us an idea of how everyday life in Lübeck used to be.

ST. ANNEN-MUSEUM **115**

ZWISCHEN HAFEN UND BURG
BETWEEN PORT AND CASTLE

Im Norden der Altstadtinsel entstanden im 13. Jahrhundert die heute noch vorhandenen Befestigungen des Burgtors und dahinter das Burgkloster. Die wehrhafte Architektur mit hohen, abweisenden Mauern aus Backstein hat das 2015 eröffnete Europäische Hansemuseum übernommen – aber stets geöffnete Durchgänge und eine Dachterrasse mit Blick auf Lübecks maritimes Erbe haben den Bau zum Anziehungspunkt gemacht.

The fortified Castle Gate and the Burgkloster Dominican friary at the north end of Altstadt were built in the 13th century and are still standing to this day. The European Hansemuseum, opened in 2015, features the same fortified architecture with high, forbidding brick walls. Permanently accessible passageways and a rooftop terrace with a view of Lübeck port have made the building a popular attraction.

VON DER HANSE ERZÄHLEN / *EXPLORING THE HANSA*

Eine wirtschaftliche und politische Gemeinschaft, die sich seit dem 13. Jahrhundert von Lübeck und Hamburg aus entwickelte, um ihre Handelswege zu sichern und ihren Einfluss zu vergrößern: Das war die Hanse, deren anerkanntes Haupt Lübeck lange war. Das Europäische Hansemuseum widmet sich mit vielfältigen Erzählformen ihrer Geschichte und den Beziehungen von Städten und Staaten in Nordeuropa, es verbindet die historische Perspektive mit dem Blick auf das Europa von heute.

Lübeck was the capital of the Hanseatic League, a commercial and political confederation founded by merchants in Lübeck and Hamburg in the 13th century to protect trade routes and expand their influence. The European Hansemuseum is dedicated to its history and the trade relations between northern European towns and states. It uses a variety of narrative forms to merge the historical perspective with a view of Europe today.

MÖNCHE UNTER SICH / *MONKS AT HOME*

Anders als das St. Annen-Kloster ist das Burgkloster leer: Die Säle selbst sind, abgesehen von wenigen alten Skulpturen und den ins Gespräch vertieften Dominikanermönchen, das Kunstwerk. Nach der Reformation dienten die Räume des aufgelösten Klosters als Armenwohnungen, später für das Lübecker Gericht, für Wechselausstellungen, in jüngerer Zeit vorübergehend als archäologisches Museum, bis dieses räumlich mit dem Europäischen Hansemuseum verbunden wurde.

Unlike St. Anne's Monastery, the Burgkloster friary is empty, save for a few early sculptures and the occasional Dominican monk. The interiors are works of art decorated with delicate frescoes. After the Reformation, the monastery was dissolved, and became a poorhouse. It was later repurposed as the Lübeck courthouse. More recently, the building was used for special exhibitions and temporarily housed an archaeological museum whose rooms were incorporated into the European Hansemuseum.

BURGKLOSTER

DEM UNRECHT WIDERSTEHEN / *RESISTING INJUSTICE*

Den drei katholischen Priestern Johannes Prassek, Eduard Müller und Hermann Lange sowie dem evangelischen Pastor Friedrich Stellbrink wurde im Lübecker Gericht während der NS-Zeit der Prozess gemacht. Wegen ihrer öffentlich geäußerten Kritik am Regime wurden sie zum Tode verurteilt. Heute sind sie als „Lübecker Märtyrer" bekannt, die Gedenkstätten in der Lutherkirche und in der Herz-Jesu-Kirche erinnern an ihren überkonfessionellen Widerstand. Im Gericht neben dem Burgkloster sind die Gefängniszellen ein bedrückender Ort der Erinnerung an die vier Märtyrer.

During the Nazi era, three Catholic priests – Johannes Prassek, Eduard Müller, and Hermann Lange – as well as the Protestant pastor Friedrich Stellbrink, were tried in the Lübeck courthouse and executed for publicly criticising the regime. Today, they are known as the 'Lübeck Martyrs', and memorials in the Luther Church and the Sacred Heart Church commemorate their resistance. The jail cells in the courthouse next to the Burgkloster friary serve as a sombre reminder of the fate of the four martyrs.

LÜBECKER MÄRTYRER 123

EIN HAUS FÜR WILLY / *A HOUSE FOR WILLY*

1933 musste Willy Brandt seine Heimatstadt verlassen, um nicht den Nationalsozialisten in die Hände zu fallen. 1972 erhielt er, inzwischen Bundeskanzler und Träger des Friedensnobelpreises, die Ehrenbürgerwürde der Hansestadt. In der Königstraße dokumentiert das Willy-Brandt-Haus das Leben des Politikers und die mit seiner Biografie verbundene Zeitgeschichte des 20. Jahrhunderts.

In 1933, Willy Brandt fled his hometown to escape the Nazis. In 1972 – by then Chancellor and Nobel Peace Prize laureate – he was made a freeman of the city. The Willy Brandt House, located in Königstrasse, documents the life of the politician and historical events of the 20th century associated with his life.

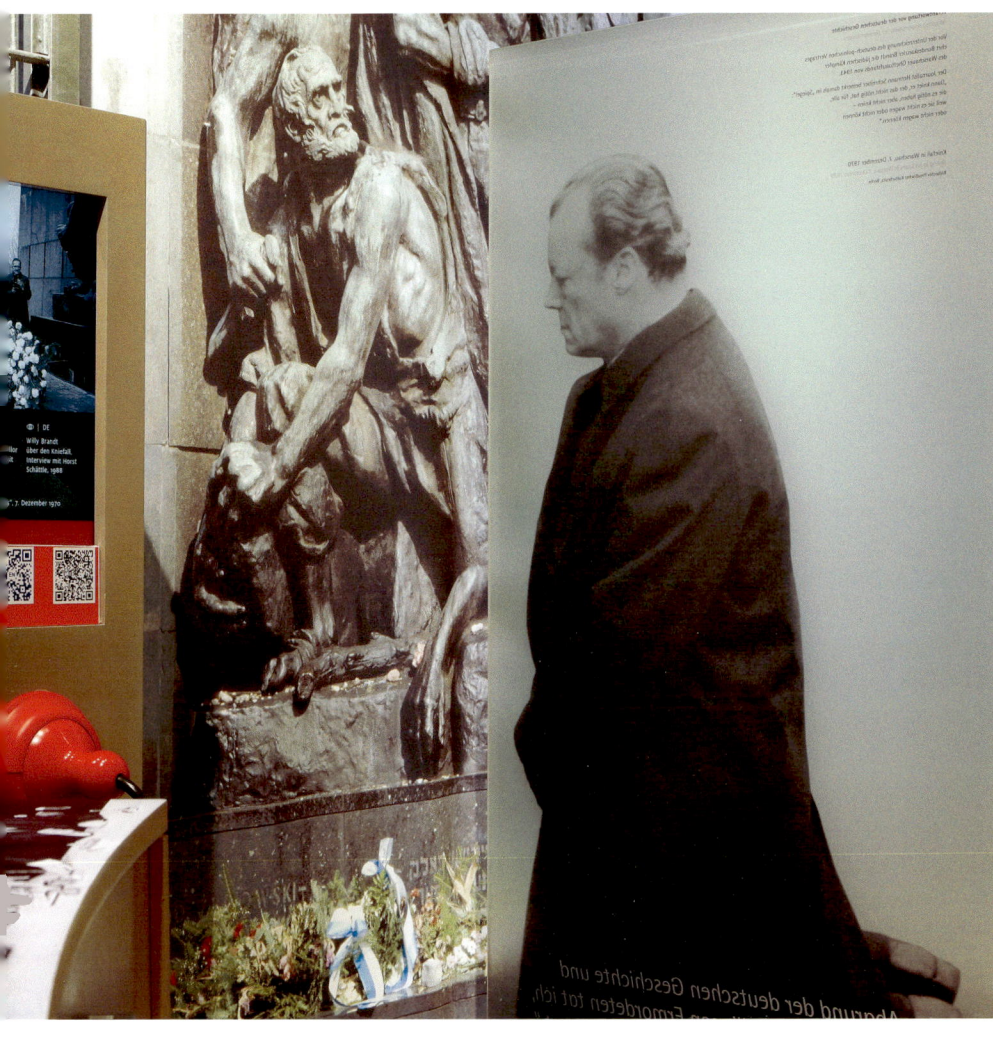

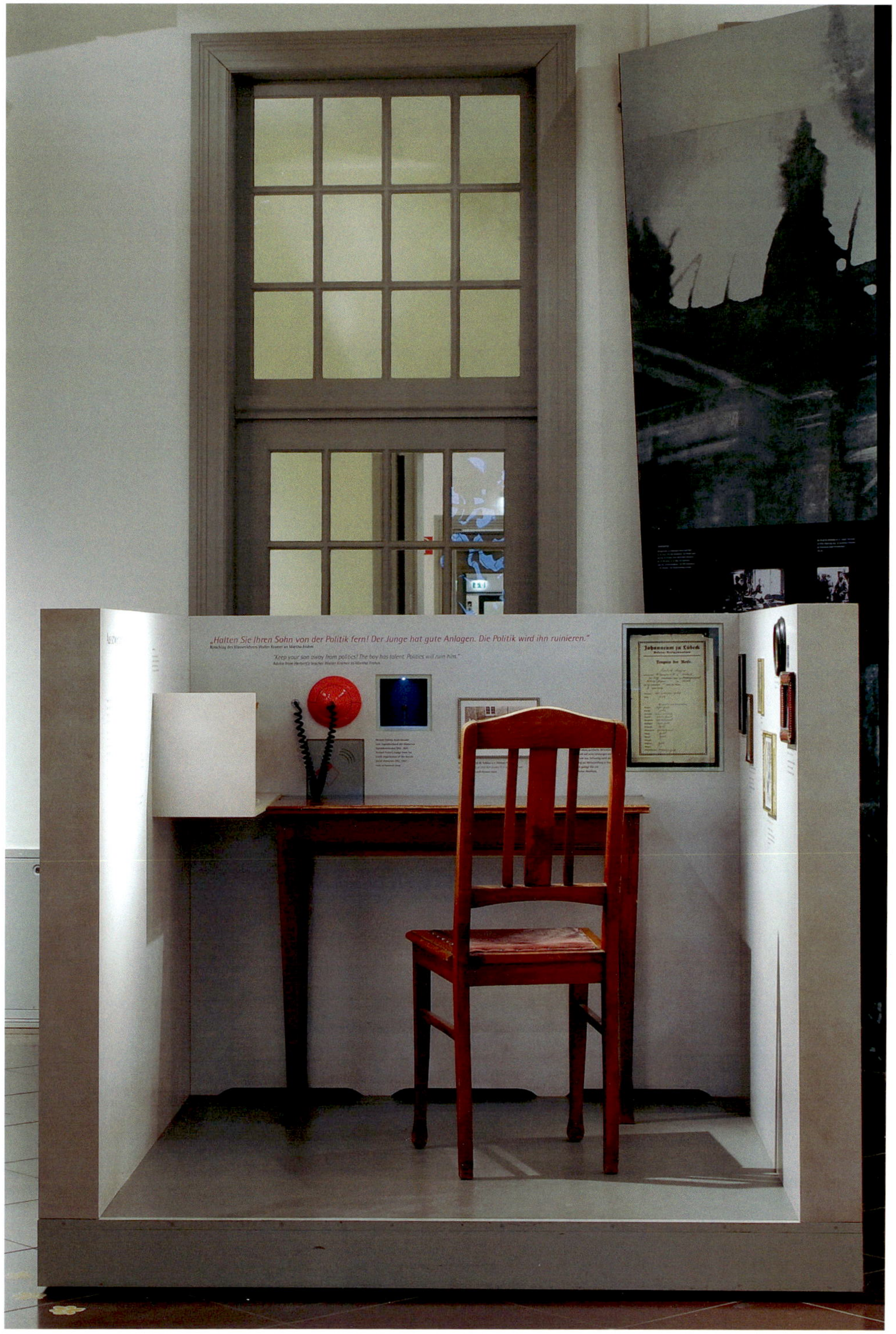
„Halten Sie Ihren Sohn von der Politik fern! Der Junge hat gute Anlagen. Die Politik wird ihn ruinieren."
"Keep your son away from politics! The boy has talent. Politics will ruin him."

ERBE DER ARBEIT / *A TRIBUTE TO THE WORKING WORLD*

Fast restlos verschwunden sind die Zeugnisse der Schwerindustrie, die es entlang der Trave in den Stadtteilen Herrenwyk, Siems und Dänischburg im 20. Jahrhundert gegeben hat. Das Hochofenwerk, die Werft der Flenderwerke, ein Kohlekraftwerk, ein Guano- und ein Fliesenwerk bildeten die Arbeitswelt für Tausende Menschen und den Lebensbezug ihrer Familien. Im ehemaligen Kaufhaus des Hochofenwerks sind die Relikte schwerer Industriearbeit und Sonderausstellungen zu sehen.

Nearly all traces of the heavy industry that once existed along the Trave River in the Herrenwyk, Siems, and Dänischburg suburbs have vanished. The blast furnace plant, the Flender shipyard, a coal-fired power plant, a fertiliser factory and a tile factory provided work and sustenance for thousands of families. Relics of the era and special exhibitions are housed in the former warehouse of the blast furnace plant.

KONZERTE UNTERM KRAN / *UNDER THE CRANE*

Einst war er der Goliath im Lübecker Hafen, der historische Drehkran von 1893 auf der nördlichen Wallhalbinsel. Mit dem Strandsalon wurde dort neues Leben auf der Kaispitze geschaffen. Die vielköpfige Band „Max and Friends" sorgt mit ihren souligen Grooves unter freiem Himmel regelmäßig für ausverkaufte Konzerte und beste Stimmung mit Blick auf Krane und Kirchen.

This old slewing crane, built in 1893 on the Northern Wall Peninsula, used to dominate the skyline of Lübeck Port. Today, Strandsalon has brought new life to the quay. Max and Friends, a large soul and groove band, regularly hold sold-out open-air concerts that give off great vibes against a backdrop of cranes and churches.

GOLDENES LICHT / *GOLDEN LIGHT*

Hafenkrane recken sich in den warmen Abendhimmel. Die historischen Hafenkrane, die auf der nördlichen Wallhalbinsel im Ruhestand vereint sind, stehen als Industriedenkmäler still, andere Krane auf dem Gelände der früheren Werft LMG heben auch heute ihre Lasten – und vereinen sich mit den Türmen der Altstadt zu einem geometrischen Puzzle.

Harbour cranes stretch out against the warm evening sky. The historic cranes on the Northern Wall Peninsula stand idle, monuments to a long-gone industrial age. Other cranes on the site of the former LMG shipyard continue to carry their loads – their silhouettes blending with that of the Altstadt churches.

HAFENABEND / *THE PORT AT DUSK*

Die Abendsonne bringt die Rottöne an der Untertrave zum Leuchten: das Signalrot des historischen Feuerschiffs *Fehmarnbelt* und das Schwedenrot des Schuppen 6, der heute als Raum für Konzerte und Veranstaltungen dient. Davor liegt der betagte Motorschlepper *Titan*, gebaut 1910 in Hamburg und seit 1937 im Lübecker Hafen zuhause.

The reds of the Lower Trave aglow in the light of the setting sun – the bright red of the historic Fehmarnbelt lightship and the falu red of Dockers' Shed 6, which now serves as a venue for concerts and events. Moored in front is the old motor tug Titan, built in Hamburg in 1910 and at home in Lübeck since 1937.

MUSEUMSHAFEN

ALTES EISEN ROSTET / *RUSTY IRON*

Lübecks maritimes Erbe steht und schwimmt als frei zu besichtigendes Hafenmuseum unter offenem Himmel – Nässe und Schmutz setzen ihm zu. Also heißt es entrosten, streichen, putzen – watt mutt, datt mutt. Oliver Schmidt, Kapitän der *Fehmarnbelt*, sorgt für freien Durchblick von der Brücke des pensionierten, aber fahrbereiten Feuerschiffs.

Lübeck's maritime heritage floats under open skies, but humidity and corrosion take their toll. Removing rust, cleaning, and painting are everyday chores. Oliver Schmidt, captain of the Fehmarnbelt, makes sure that the view from the bridge of the decommissioned but still-operational lightship stays clear.

ANS WASSER ODER AUFS WASSER? / *BY THE WATER OR ON THE WATER?*

Hektisch wird es im Stadthafen an der Untertrave höchstens, wenn ein Drachenboot seine Zähne zeigt. Alle anderen Wasserfahrzeuge tuckern, paddeln, rudern oder gleiten gemächlich vorbei. Denn meistens ist der Weg auch das Ziel und Eile fehl am Drehbrückenplatz.

The only time things get hectic at the seaport on the Lower Trave is when a dragon boat shows up. All other watercraft that pass here chug, paddle, row, or glide past at a leisurely pace. Most of the time, the journey is more important than the destination. Similarly, nobody is in a hurry on Drehbrückenplatz, a laid-back square in the port.

HAFEN AN DER UNTERTRAVE

IM ZEICHEN DES ADLERS / *FOR THE GLORY OF LÜBECK*

Ihr Liegeplatz ist die nördliche Wallhalbinsel, aber als seetüchtige Botschafterin Lübecks ist die *Lisa von Lübeck*, der Nachbau einer Kraweel aus dem 15. Jahrhundert, auch auf der Ostsee unterwegs. Von 1999 bis 2004 haben 350 Menschen, unter ihnen viele Jugendliche, am Bau des Schiffes mitgewirkt. Bei Gästefahrten lässt sich auf der *Lisa*, benannt nach der Mäzenin Lisa Dräger, in historischem Ambiente Seeluft schnuppern.

Her home port is the Northern Wall Peninsula, but as a seaworthy ambassador of Lübeck, the Lisa von Lübeck, a reconstructed 15th-century caravel, also sails the Baltic Sea. From 1999 to 2004, 350 people, including many youngsters, helped build the ship. Excursions on the Lisa, named after the project's initiator, Lisa Dräger, allow passengers to enjoy the sea air in a historical setting.

LISA VON LÜBECK

KIRCHE MIT KUGELN / *THE CHURCH WITH THE SPHERES*

Der Turm von St. Jakobi überragt die nördliche Altstadt und den Hafen, mit dem die Kirche eng verbunden ist. Die Schmucklust des Barocks ist an vielen Details zu erkennen: Der Dachreiter und die Kugeln datieren aus dem 17., die Uhr, die nur einen Zeiger hat, aus dem 18. Jahrhundert. Aber das genügte, auf Minuten kam es nicht an – zumal es ja auch noch die Stundenglocke gab (und gibt).

The steeple of St. Jacob's Church overlooks the northern part of the Altstadt and the port. The church is closely connected to Lübeck's seafaring life, and its ornate and elaborate décor is baroque in style. The ridge turret and spheres date back to the 17th century, and the clock, which is from the 18th century, has only one hand. Back then, minutes were of no importance – what counted (and still does) was the hourly bell.

BAROCK IN HÜLLE UND FÜLLE / *BAROQUE JEWEL*

St. Jakobi hat den Zweiten Weltkrieg unzerstört überstanden. Deshalb bestimmt die barocke Üppigkeit auch das Kircheninnere: von den beiden Orgelprospekten über den hochaufragenden Altar bis zu den vielen Epitaphien. Dazwischen prunkt noch Gotik hervor, besonders beeindruckend mit den gemalten Heiligenfiguren an den Säulen.

St. Jacob's survived World War II undamaged, and its exquisite baroque interior was preserved – from the two organ façades to its high altar and the many epitaphs on the walls. Gothic architectural elements are also still very much in evidence, such as the impressive frescos of saints that decorate the pillars.

GEDENKEN IM WANDEL / *A CHANGE OF PERSPECTIVE*

Das Ehrenmal des Bildhauers Fritz Behn von 1921 hat mit der Überformung durch die Künstlerin Maria Moser einen Bedeutungswandel erfahren: Nicht mehr der Soldat soll verehrt werden, er wird verdeckt von einem flammend bunten Tuch. Das Gedenken an die Opfer von Kriegsgewalt findet nun vor dem Kreuz statt, behält aber seinen historischen Hintergrund.

The memorial created by sculptor Fritz Behn in 1921 took on a new perspective after being redesigned by artist Maria Moser. It no longer honours the soldier; instead, it commemorates the victims of war with a cross made of fabric painted in flaming colours. It conceals the original sculpture while retaining the memorial's historical context.

SEEFAHRT BRINGT AUCH NOT
THE SEAFARERS' CHURCH

Schiffsbilder und Glasfenster erinnern in St. Jakobi an die Seefahrt und an Schiffsunglücke Lübecker Seeleute. Die Kapelle, in der das geborstene Rettungsboot der Viermastbark *Pamir* liegt, ist heute nationale Gedenkstätte für die zivile Seefahrt.

The maritime motifs and stained-glass windows of St. Jacob's remind visitors of the seafarers from Lübeck and the shipwrecks they suffered. The chapel, where the wrecked lifeboat of the four-master barque Pamir is on display, is now the National Memorial of the Merchant Navy.

150 ORGELN

STADT DER ORGELN / *CITY OF ORGANS*

Es sind die Orgeln, die Lübeck zu einer Metropole der Kirchenmusik machen. Auf dem Bild ganz links prunkt die Orgel von St. Aegidien, und St. Jakobi hat gleich zwei: die Große Orgel mit dem bis unter das Gewölbe ragenden Prospekt und die Kleine Orgel im nördlichen Seitenschiff. Die ältesten Elemente beider Orgeln stammen noch aus dem 15. Jahrhundert, die Ansicht wird durch die Erweiterungen des 17. Jahrhunderts bestimmt, zu denen die grotesken Gesichter auf den Pfeifen gehören.

It's the organs that make Lübeck a centre of church music. Pictured on the far left is the magnificent organ of the Church of St. Aegidien, and St. Jacob's (centre) has two: the main organ with a façade that reaches up to the vault and the small organ on the north wall. The oldest elements of both organs date back to the 15th century. They owe their current appearance to extensions carried out in the 17th century, including the golden faces painted on the flue pipes.

MUSIKALISCHE OASE / *MUSICAL FOREST RETREAT*

Mitten im Wesloer Forst liegt das Waldzimmer – in einem Haus der früheren Waldschule, wo Lübecker Stadtkinder Unterricht und Erholung inmitten der Natur erhielten. Jetzt wächst hier, erfunden und entwickelt vom Musiker Florian Galow, ein kreatives Kleinod für Konzerte, Aufnahmen und andere Veranstaltungen heran, die den Weg in den Wald lohnen.

The Waldzimmer is in the middle of Wesloe Forest, in the former forest school, where Lübeck's children enjoyed classes and recreation in natural surroundings. Initiated and developed by musician Florian Galow, a creative gem of a venue is emerging with space for concerts, recordings, and other events, making it well worth the excursion to the forest.

WALDZIMMER

BEATS IN DER BURG / *BEATS IN THE CASTLE*

Leben und Arbeiten unter einem Dach – aber was für einem. Der Schlagzeuger Max Zeidler wohnt mit seiner Familie am und im Burgtor, und hier unterrichtet er auch. Mit seiner Musik steht er für eine kreative Tradition in den historischen Räumen, denn hier waren schon die Schriftstellerin Ida Boyd, die Weberinnen Ruth Löbe und Alen Müller-Hellwig sowie deren Mann, der Geigenbauer Günter Hellwig, tätig.

Living and working under one roof – but what a roof. Drummer Max Zeidler lives with his family in the Castle Gate, and he also teaches music there. With his music, he is part of a creative tradition in these historic rooms, following in the footsteps of writer Ida Boyd, craft weavers Ruth Löbe and Alen Müller-Hellwig, and violinmaker Günter Hellwig.

DRUMBURG IM BURGTOR 155

STILVOLL STUDIEREN / *STUDYING IN STYLE*

In einem großen Ensemble wertvoller Kaufmannshäuser und ehemaliger Speicher zwischen der Großen Petersgrube und der Depenau hat die Musikhochschule ihr Domizil. Studierende und Lehrende aus aller Welt machen sie zu einem Ort internationaler Begegnung und Zusammenarbeit. Das gusseiserne Paar schmückt eine Haustür der Musikhochschule – was die beiden sich wohl zu erzählen haben?

The Academy of Music is housed in a large ensemble of historical merchants' houses and former warehouses between Grosse Petersgrube and Depenau. Students and teachers from all over the world make it a centre for international encounter and collaboration. A cast-iron couple adorns the academy's front gate – what secrets do they hold?

MUSIKHOCHSCHULE

ALTE HALLEN NEU BELEBT / *OLD HALLS COME ALIVE*

Früher dröhnten hier Maschinen und Niethämmer: Wo ein Jahrhundert lang Schwimmbagger und Schiffe gebaut wurden, ertönen heute klassische Musik, Heavy Metal, Pop und Jazz. Aus dem Industriebetrieb der Lübecker Maschinenbau Gesellschaft ist in den letzten Jahren die Kulturwerft geworden, mit viel Platz für Konzerte, Feiern, Ateliers, Ausstellungen und Messen. Auch die Musikhochschule nutzt das Areal für Konzerte.

For a century, these boatbuilding halls reverberated with the roar of machines and rivet hammers; today, they are filled with the sound of classical music, heavy metal, pop, and jazz. In recent years, the industrial site of the Lübecker Maschinenbau Gesellschaft (LMG) has been converted into the Kulturwerft, offering plenty of space for concerts, events, studios, exhibitions, and trade fairs. Even the Academy of Music uses the venue for concerts.

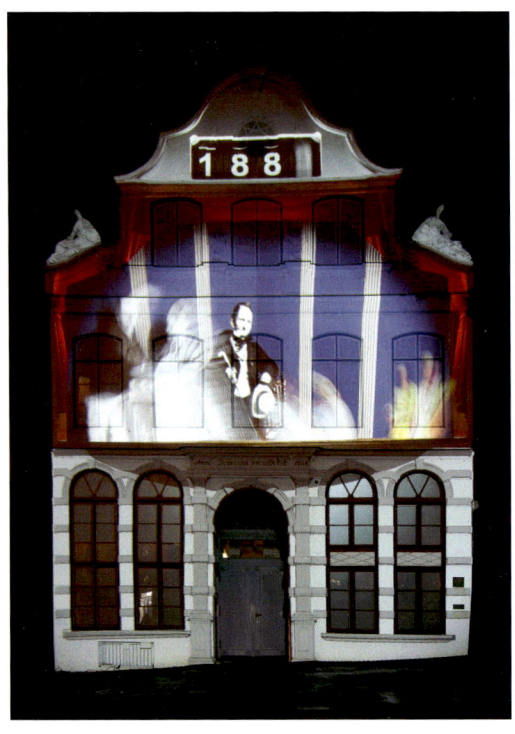

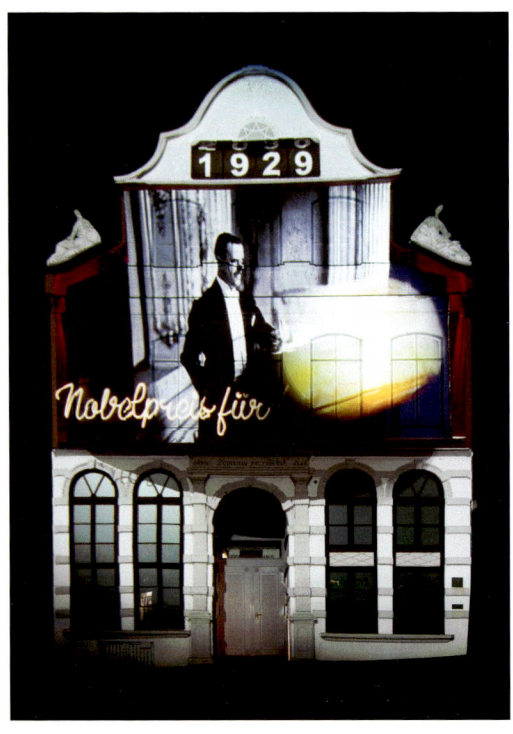

160　BUDDENBROOKHAUS

EIN HAUS ALS BUCH / *A HOUSE LIKE A BOOK*

Lübecks bekanntestes Haus ist für einige Jahre nur Fassade. Dahinter entsteht der Neubau für das Literaturmuseum, in dem sich alles um Leben und Werk der Schriftstellerbrüder Heinrich und Thomas Mann dreht. In der Wartezeit dient die Fassade als Bilderbuch: Eine Videoinstallation zeigt wichtige Momente aus der Geschichte des Hauses, ein Comic erzählt von dem, was kommen wird.

Over the next few years, only the façade of Lübeck's most famous house will be accessible to the public while the new Literary Museum, dedicated to the life and work of the writers Heinrich and Thomas Mann, is under construction. In the meantime, the façade has been transformed into a picture book. A video installation highlights key moments of the building's history, and a comic strip illustrates what the future will bring.

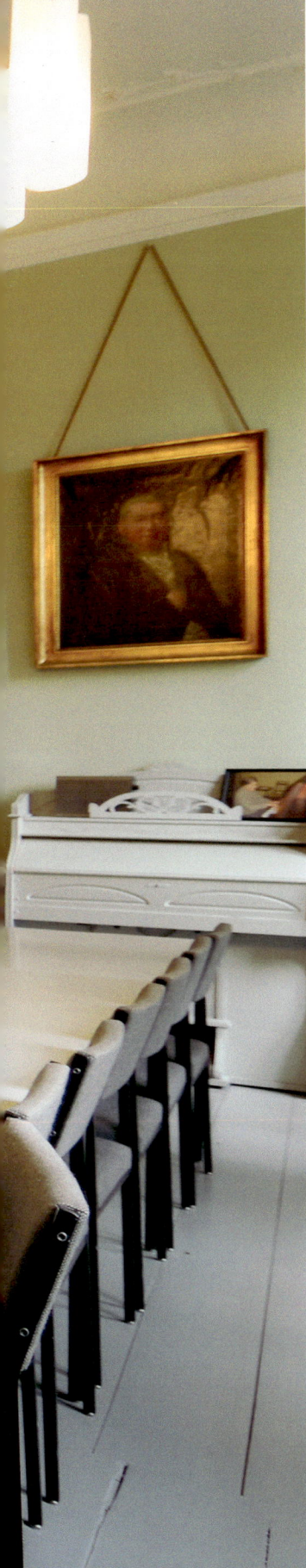

VERSTECKTES WISSEN / *HIDDEN KNOWLEDGE*

Es ist einer von jenen Räumen auf der Altstadtinsel, die immer da, aber weitgehend unbekannt sind. Ein stiller Raum in der Reformierten Kirche, in dem die umfangreiche Bibliothek des Theologen Otto Friedrich Butendach aus dem 18. Jahrhundert steht. Zwischen und über den Büchern nehmen die Prediger der Reformierten Gemeinde die im Raum Anwesenden still und würdevoll in den Blick.

This is one of those lesser-known gems of the Altstadt. The Butendach Library is a quiet room in the Reformed Church containing the extensive library of 18th-century theologian Otto Friedrich Butendach. From their places on the walls, dignified clergymen of the Reformed Church look down serenely at visitors to the library.

VOM KLOSTER ZUR STADTBIBLOTHEK / *FROM MONASTERY TO PUBLIC LIBRARY*

„… libraria pressa stat ista via" – eine Bibliothek steht nahe dieser Straße: So heißt es in einer steinernen Inschrift im ehemaligen Katharinenkloster, in dem die Stadtbibliothek ansässig ist. Die Kloster- und Kirchenbibliotheken des Mittelalters bilden den Grundstock der öffentlichen Bibliothek Lübecks. Der nach einem Historiker benannte Mantelssaal gehört zu den sehenswerten historischen Räumen. Die Schnitzfigur an einem Gestühl in St. Jakobi zeigt einen lesenden Theologen.

Libraria pressa stat ista via – a library stands near this street – reads the inscription set in stone in the public library, formerly St. Catherine's Monastery. The monastic and church libraries of the Middle Ages form the foundation of Lübeck's modern public library. The Mantelssaal, named after a historian, is one of the historic rooms worth visiting. A figure carved on a pew in St. Jacob's shows a cleric reading.

SCHARBAUS SCHÄTZE
SCHARBAU'S TREASURES

Wo früher die Mönche des Katharinenklosters schliefen, haben heute historische Buchbestände ihre Ruhe, sofern der heutige Scharbausaal nicht für Führungen oder Veranstaltungen geöffnet ist. Benannt ist der gotische Saal nach dem bibliophilen Theologen Heinrich Scharbau, der seine Büchersammlung der Bibliothek vermachte. Die Regale entlang der Wände gehören zur Erstmöblierung der Bibliothek im 17. Jahrhundert, Gemälde zeigen Reformatoren und Bibliothekare.

Historical book collections rest quietly where the monks of St. Catherine's Monastery used to sleep – unless Scharbau Hall is open for guided tours or events. The Gothic Hall is named after theologian Heinrich Scharbau, who bequeathed his book collection to the library. The hall retains its original bookshelves from the 17th century, with portraits of reformers and librarians on the walls.

168   GÜNTER GRASS-HAUS

KUNST UND KOLONIALWAREN
ART AND COLONIAL GOODS

Der bunt gefüllte Krämerladen im Günter Grass-Haus in der Glockengießerstraße inszeniert den Ort, an dem die *Blechtrommel* spielt – der Nachkriegsroman, für den der Schriftsteller den Nobelpreis erhielt. Auf abwechslungsreiche Weise macht das Haus Literatur anschaubar und erlebbar. Grafiken und Skulpturen des vielseitigen Künstlers Grass füllen Haus und Garten.

The general store in the Günter Grass House in Glockengiesserstrasse recreates the setting of The Tin Drum – the post-war novel for which Günter Grass received the Nobel Prize for Literature. The house makes literature come alive in a variety of ways. The house and garden are full of drawings and sculptures by the multi-talented artist.

GÜNTER GRASS-HAUS **169**

HEIM AN DIE OSTSEE
AT HOME ON THE BALTIC SEA

1995 entschied sich Günter Grass, sein Büro nach Lübeck zu verlegen, das durch die Ostsee mit seiner Heimatstadt Danzig verbunden ist. Heute hat auch die Stiftung, die seinen künstlerischen Nachlass betreut, ihren Sitz im Günter Grass-Haus. Zeitgenössische Kunst – auch von Günter Grass – verwahrt und verkauft Galerist Frank-Thomas Gaulin seit vielen Jahrzehnten in einem Dielenhaus in der Königstraße.

In 1995, Günter Grass decided to move his office to Lübeck, which is connected to his hometown of Danzig (now Gdansk in Poland) by the Baltic Sea. Today, the foundation that looks after his estate is housed in the Günter Grass House. Frank-Thomas Gaulin has for many decades collected and sold contemporary art in his gallery on Königstrasse, including works by Günter Grass.

170   GÜNTER UND UTE GRASS STIFTUNG / KUNSTHAUS

DURCHBLICKE / *INSIGHTS*

Sprossenfenster erlauben den Blick auf plastische Arbeiten von Günter Grass, sie füllen in den Räumen der Stiftung Tisch und Nische, träumen vor sich hin oder halten einander. Wer Kunstbücher sucht, wird im Antiquariat des Kunsthauses fündig, wo die Bücher jeden Zentimeter der hohen Regale füllen, Bilder Kisten und den Boden einnehmen und kaum noch Platz für Antiquar Klaus Oestmann lassen.

A peek through the foundation's windows offers a glimpse of rooms full of sculptural figures by Günter Grass. If you are looking for art books, you will find them at the Kunsthaus, in the antiquarian bookshop. Books fill every inch of the walls from floor to ceiling, and paintings and lithographs overflow from boxes and cover the floor, leaving very little space for antiquarian Klaus Oestmann to move.

GÜNTER UND UTE GRASS STIFTUNG / ANTIQUARIAT IM KUNSTHAUS

174 MUSEUM BEHNHAUS DRÄGERHAUS

EDLE WEITLÄUFIGKEIT
NOBLE SPACIOUSNESS

Platz ist der wahre Luxus – das wusste auch schon Lübecks Großbürgertum. Seit dem 18. Jahrhundert ließ man altertümliche Häuser mit neuer Pracht umbauen – und besonders vornehm das Behnhaus, benannt nach der Bürgermeisterfamilie, die das Haus bis 1921 besaß. Von der weitläufigen Galerie kann der Blick in Zimmerfluchten, über Treppen und Kunstwerke schweifen, über Gemälde und Skulpturen.

Space is true luxury. Lübeck's gentry was well aware of that. From the 18th century onwards, they restored old buildings, creating magnificent townhouses, and the Behnhaus – named after a mayor whose family owned the house until 1921 – is a particularly elegant example. From the generously proportioned gallery, the visitor's gaze wanders over corridors, staircases, paintings, sculptures, and other works of art.

RUNDE GESCHICHTE / *SUCCESSFUL ALLROUND*

Lübecks bekanntestes Bauwerk steht schief. Das Holstentor hat nie Feinde abwehren müssen, gefährdet war es mehr durch die eigenen Bürger der Stadt. Denn die wollten Mitte des 19. Jahrhunderts das unnütze Verkehrshindernis abreißen lassen. Es wurde gerettet, es wurde berühmt – und ist heute ein Stadtmuseum. Zu bestaunen ist darin das Stadtmodell von 1934, das auch den eindrucksvollen Befestigungsring zeigt.

Lübeck's most famous building has leaning towers. The Holsten Gate has never had to fend off enemies; the city's own citizens were more of a danger. In the mid-19th century, they wanted to demolish it because it was considered a nuisance to traffic. The gate was saved and became famous. Today, it houses the Holstentor Museum. Visitors can admire a model of the city created in 1934, which also shows its impressive ring of fortifications.

MÄCHTIGE MAUERN / *MIGHTY WALLS*

Backstein nicht zu knapp. Als der damalige Stadtherr, der dänische König, die hohe Stadtmauer im frühen 13. Jahrhundert errichten ließ, gab es weit und breit kein vergleichbares Bauwerk. Menschen, die von Norden das Burgtor erreichten, waren beeindruckt.

No lack of bricks. When the Danish king who ruled Lübeck at the time had the high city wall built in the early 13th century, there was no other such structure far and wide. Everyone who approached Castle Gate from the north was duly impressed.

180　HUBBRÜCKE / DREHBRÜCKE

BEWEGLICHE DENKMÄLER / *WORKING MONUMENTS*

Viele Bauten zeugen auch heute noch vom Ausbau des Hafens in den Jahren um 1900. Dazu gehören als technische Denkmäler die Hubbrücke über den Elbe-Lübeck-Kanal (links) und die Drehbrücke über die Trave. Mit fortgerücktem Alter zeigen sie sich manchmal kapriziös und bewegen sich nicht wie vorgesehen. Dann ist Geduld oder ein Umweg gefragt.

Many structures still standing were built when the port was expanded around 1900. These include important technical breakthroughs, such as the lift bridge over the Elbe-Lübeck Canal (left) and the swing bridge over the Trave. The older they get, the more capricious they become and do not function as intended. That calls for patience or a detour.

WEGE IM GRÜNEN / GREEN SPACES

Wasserflächen und Reste der alten Wallanlagen umgeben die Altstadtinsel. Sie bieten zahlreiche Ausblicke und wechselnde Perspektiven, von denen sich manche erst im Herbst entfalten, wenn die vielen Bäume ihre Blätter verlieren. Spazieren, Joggen und Radfahren geht hier zu jeder Jahreszeit – ganz ungestört vom motorisierten Verkehr.

Waterways, ponds, and remnants of the old ramparts surround the island that comprises the old city of Lübeck. Visitors can relax and enjoy the changing vistas, some of which unfold only in autumn when the trees shed their leaves. It's possible to walk, jog and cycle year-round – completely undisturbed by traffic.

BUNTES REFUGIUM / *A COLOURFUL REFUGE*

Als Lehrgarten für den Schulunterricht öffnete der Schulgarten auf der Falkenwiese 1930 zum ersten Mal seine Pforten. Diesem Zweck dient er auch heute noch, ein wichtiger Fokus liegt auf ökologischer Bildung. Mit einem kleinen Café und musikalischen Veranstaltungen ist der Schulgarten aber auch zum blühenden Treffpunkt für andere Generationen geworden.

The School Garden on Falkenwiese opened its doors for the first time in 1930 as an educational garden for schoolchildren. It still serves this purpose today, with a strong focus on environmental education. The School Garden has a small café and hosts musical events, making it a popular meeting place for other generations as well.

EINTRÄCHTIGE STILLE
PEACE AND TRANQUILITY

An manchen Orten in der Altstadt ist es eng, und Mauern begrenzen den Blick. Weitläufig aber sind die Kirchhöfe, die früher als Friedhöfe dienten. Besonders ausgedehnt ist der Domkirchhof mit seiner Lutherbuche. Großzügig sind auch die Bürgergärten hinter den großen Häusern in der Königstraße. Im Garten des Behnhauses stehen Skulpturen von einer besonderen stillen Ausdruckskraft.

Streets in the old city tend to be narrow, and its walls block the view. But the churchyards, which used to be graveyards, are spacious. One of the largest is the cathedral churchyard with its mighty beech planted in honour of Martin Luther. The gardens behind the large townhouses in Königstrasse are also quite spacious. The Behnhaus garden features sculptures that exude a serene charm.

BIOTOP MIT GESCHICHTE / *A BIOTOPE WITH A LONG HISTORY*

Schon seit der Stadtgründung staut der Mühlendamm das Wasser der Wakenitz kurz bevor es die Trave erreicht. Der Mühlenteich lieferte Energie für mehrere nebeneinander liegende Wassermühlen – zwei stehen noch – und schützte die Stadt. Zugleich spiegelt der Teich den wuchtigen Dom. Die Wasservögel interessiert all das nicht, ihnen ist der Teich Ort für Balz und Brut.

When Lübeck was founded, the river Wakenitz was dammed just before it reached the Trave, forming the Mühlenteich. This mill pond fed several watermills on the Mühlendamm, of which two still exist today, and protected the city. The pond mirrors Lübeck's mighty cathedral, but the water birds take no notice; for them, a pond is the place to mate and breed.

MÜHLENTEICH UND DOM

BEIEINANDER DER ZEITALTER / *VIEWS OF AGES PAST*

Im Abendrot streift der Blick am St. Annen-Museum vorbei auf die Domtürme. Gleich wird auch die Gaslaterne erglühen und wie seit über 160 Jahren für ein warmes Nachtlicht sorgen. Das prähistorische Walskelett ruht als Exponat des Museums für Natur und Umwelt unter Glas im Hof des ehemaligen Domklosters.

The silhouettes of St. Anne's Museum and the cathedral spires juxtaposed against the sky at dusk. In a moment, the gas lamp will cast a warm glow, as it has for over 160 years. The skeleton of a prehistoric whale encased in glass in the courtyard of the former cathedral monastery is an exhibit of the Museum of Nature and the Environment.

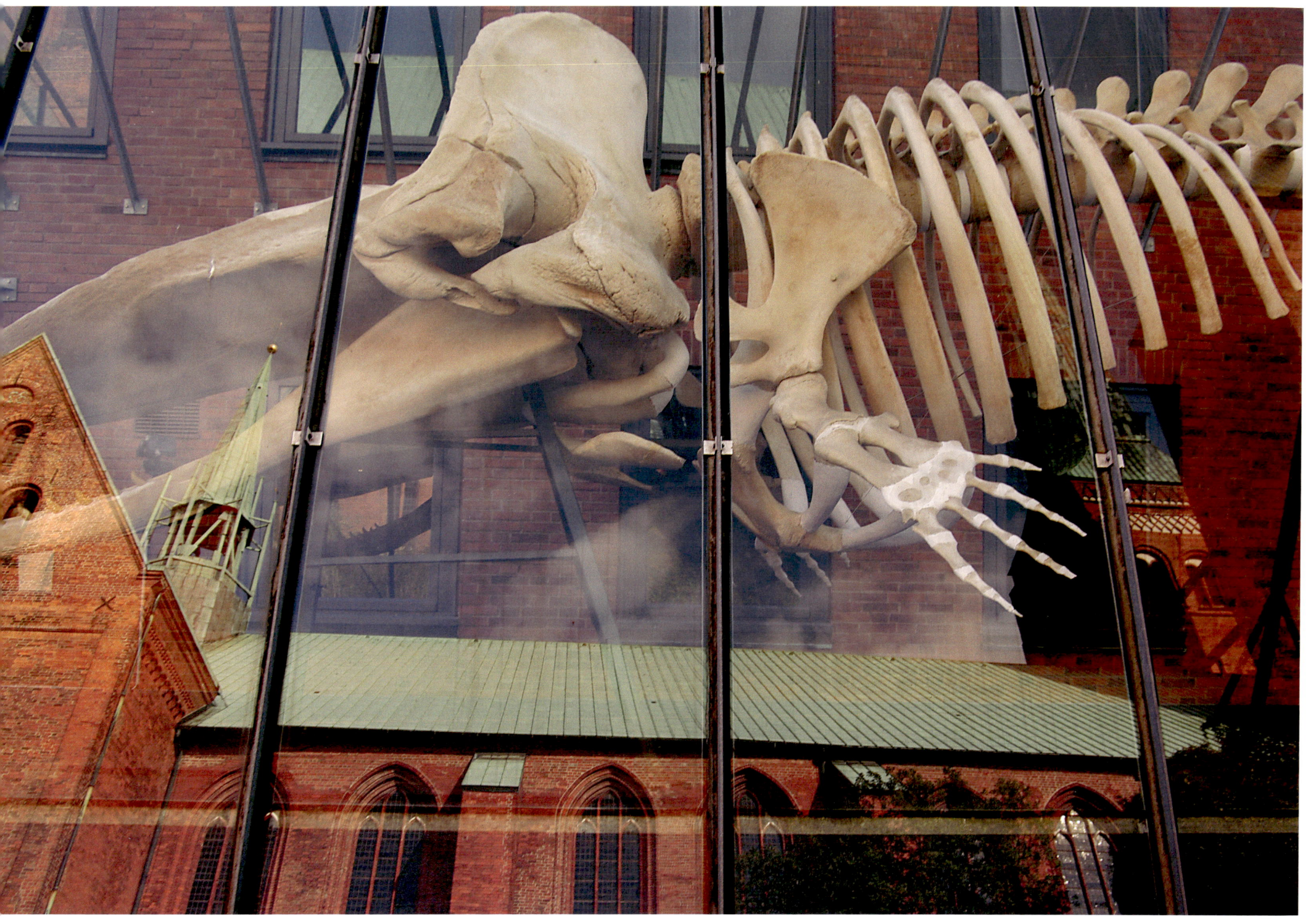

DOM / MUSEUM FÜR NATUR UND UMWELT

192 SALZSPEICHER / SIEBENTE QUERSTRASSE

HERBSTNEBEL / *AUTUMN FOG*

Da glüht sie, die Laterne in der Siebenten Querstraße, und wärmt zumindest die Augen. Die Erste bis Sechste Querstraße sucht man vergeblich, denn statt „Siebente" hieß es im Mittelalter „Zoghe", auf Hochdeutsch „Sau": Der Straßenname bezog sich vermutlich auf Schweine, die hier von einem Bäcker gehalten wurden. Die Möwen sorgen ganzjährig für einen maritimen Klang an Trave und Salzspeicher.

The glow of the gas lamp in Siebente Querstrasse (literally, seventh cross street) is a warming sight. But there's no use trying to find the first to sixth cross streets because, in the Middle Ages, instead of Siebente, the cross street was called Zoghe, or Sau in standard German. The street name probably referred to pigs kept there by a baker. The seagulls wheeling above the salt warehouses and Trave river give the city a year-round coastal feel.

KRIMI AN DER HAFENKANTE
DOCKLAND MURDER MYSTERY

Wie Glühwürmchen durchdringen die Lampen am Hafenschuppen, die Signale und die Lichter an der Hubbrücke den Nebel. Es ist Herbst, es ist feucht und es ist kühl – da zieht es auch die Lübeckerinnen und Lübecker kaum noch an die im Sommer so belebte Untertrave. Edgar Wallace lässt grüßen.

The harbour shed lamps, and the signals and the lights on the lift bridge glimmer through the fog like fireflies – the perfect setting for an Edgar Wallace crime story. It's a cold and damp autumn evening, and even the locals don't feel drawn to the Lower Trave, a spot popular in summer.

196　MENGSTRASSE / ENGELSGRUBE / KANZLEIGEBÄUDE

WENN ES DUNKEL WIRD / *NIGHTFALL*

Den Worten von Ernst Willkomm aus dem Jahr 1850 ist nichts hinzuzufügen: „Mit Sonnenuntergang erstirbt das Leben in Lübeck großentheils, nur wenige Straßen und Plätze sind bis nach zehn Uhr besucht. Allein gerade in solcher Stille der Nacht ist es interessant, Lübeck sich von allen Seiten zu betrachten. Wählt man dazu eine klare Vollmondnacht, so kann ein phantasiereicher Mensch sich glückliche Stunden bereiten …"

The words of Ernst Willkomm from 1850 describe it perfectly: "At sunset, Lübeck empties out almost completely; only a few streets and squares are still frequented after ten o'clock. But it is precisely the stillness of the night that makes it interesting to explore Lübeck's many sides. If it happens to be a clear night with a full moon, an imaginative person can pass many an enjoyable hour…"

MENGSTRASSE / ENGELSGRUBE / KANZLEIGEBÄUDE

AUF ZU NEUEM GLAUBEN
PIONEERING A NEW FAITH

Sie ist die kleinste der Altstadtkirchen, spielte aber eine herausragende Rolle bei der Einführung der Reformation in Lübeck. Ihr Prediger Andreas Wilms hatte als erster Lübecker Theologe Beziehungen zu Martin Luther und anderen Reformatoren, ihr Pastor Johann by der Erde schloss als erster eine Ehe. Mit Turm und Dach ragt St. Aegidien aus dem eng bebauten Aegidienviertel immer noch heraus.

It is the smallest of the churches in the Altstadt, but it played a prominent role in bringing the Reformation to Lübeck. Its pastor Andreas Wilms was the first theologian in Lübeck to associate with Martin Luther and other reformers, and pastor Johann by der Erde was the first clergyman in Lübeck to marry. With its tower and roof, St. Aegidien still dominates this densely built quarter.

ST. AEGIDIEN

TRAGENDE ROLLE / *A SUPPORTING ROLE*

Mächtige Balken tragen die Glocken im Turm von St. Aegidien. Die älteste wurde 1591 gegossen und wiegt drei Tonnen. Zu hören ist sie, wenn am Sonnabend alle vier Glocken zugleich als Vollgeläut ertönen. Der Dachstuhl über dem Kirchenschiff und im Turm ist vollständig aus Holz – standhaft errichtet, nachhaltig über viele Jahrhunderte.

Mighty beams support the bells in the tower of St. Aegidien. The oldest was cast in 1591 and weighs three tonnes. It can be heard on Saturdays when all four bells ring at the same time. The truss above the nave and in the tower is made entirely of wood – solid and built to last for many centuries.

202 ST. AEGIDIEN

BILDERLUST / *CARNAL TOUCHES*

Den Zweiten Weltkrieg überstand St. Aegidien fast unbeschädigt, und so blieb die reichhaltige Ausstattung aus Renaissance und Barock erhalten. Der Lettner oder Singechor von 1587 mit seinen prächtigen Schnitzereien bildet den Blickfang und lädt mit seinen vielen Details zum Bilderlesen ein – und dabei geht es nicht nur keusch zu.

St. Aegidien survived World War II almost unscathed, preserving its magnificent Renaissance and Baroque interiors. The rood screen or choir of 1587 with its splendid carvings is the church's outstanding feature. They are rich in detail – some far from chaste.

ST. AEGIDIEN

WEIHNACHTSSTADT / 'TIS THE SEASON...

Die Kirchen füllen sich mit Tannengrün und warmem Licht, dem die Kühle der Architektur eine Zeit lang weicht. Wie auf einer Bühne stehen die Holzskulpturen des Triumphkreuzes von 1477 – gleich alt wie das Holstentor – in Andacht beieinander. Beim Luftangriff 1942 schwer beschädigt, wurde es erst in den 1970er Jahren restauriert. Dabei fand sich im Finger einer Skulptur ein vierhundert Jahre alter Zettel, auf dem die Werkstatt Bernt Notkes genannt ist.

The churches are decked out in fir sprigs and warm lights, and, for a while, the austerity of their architecture recedes into the background. As if on a stage, the wooden figures of Bernt Notke's Triumphal Cross of 1477 – as old as the Holsten Gate – stand together in devotion. Badly damaged in an air raid in 1942, it was not restored until the 1970s. In the process, a 400-year-old note mentioning Notke's studio was found etched into one figure's fingers.

ST. MARIEN / DOM

206 WEIHNACHTSMARKT IM HEILIGEN-GEIST-HOSPITAL

ALTE KUNST, NEUES KUNSTHANDWERK
SACRED ART AND MODERN CRAFTS

Beim Kunsthandwerkermarkt im Heiligen-Geist-Hospital füllen sich die „Kabäuschen" mit vielfältigem Kunsthandwerk. Früher wohnten dort unter dem großen Kirchenschiff des „Langhauses" alte Menschen. Der Verein „Frau und Kultur" organisiert seit über fünfzig Jahren den Markt, für den Kenner auch per Schiff aus Skandinavien anreisen.

At the arts and crafts fair at the Hospital of the Holy Spirit, craftspeople and artisans show off their wide range of wares in cubbyholes under the large nave of the long hall, which used to house elderly people. For over 50 years, the association Frau und Kultur has organised the market. It is a popular destination, even for visitors from Scandinavia, who typically arrive by ship.

LICHTERLINIEN / *STRINGS OF LIGHT*

Auch die Lisa von Lübeck schmückt sich zur Weihnachtszeit mit Licht, während ihr gegenüber an der Hafenstraße der historische Schuppen 10/11 leuchtet. Wo im 20. Jahrhundert die Hafenarbeiter zu ihren Schichten eingeteilt wurden, locken heute gastronomische Genüsse. Hoch hinaus kommt man zur Weihnachtszeit mit dem Riesenrad auf dem Koberg.

During the Christmas season, the Lisa von Lübeck is decorated with lights, and opposite, the windows of the historic dockers' sheds in Hafenstrasse radiate a warm glow. For most of the 20th century, dockworkers were assigned their shifts here, but now guests enjoy culinary delights. The Ferris wheel at Koberg offers a bird's eye view of the sea of Christmas lights below.

WEIHNACHTSSTADT / *WINTER WONDERLAND*

Weiße Weihnachten – das ist auch in Lübeck meist nur ein Wunschtraum. Doch wenn es einmal schneit, werden Türme und Dächer der Altstadt zu einer Vorlage für ein romantisches Bilderbuch. Es wird still, wenn nur noch der Schnee unter den Füßen knirscht und er ansonsten den Lärm der Stadt verschluckt.

White Christmases are few and far between in Lübeck. But when it does snow, the city's roofs and steeples form a quintessentially romantic winter scene. The typical noises of the city appear to be smothered beneath a soft blanket, with only the sound of snow crunching underfoot to break the comforting silence.

VERGNÜGEN UNTERM STERNENZELT / *FUN UNDER A BLANKET OF STARS*

Wenn der Weihnachtsmarkt wieder abgebaut ist, steht der Markt für die Eisbahn zur Verfügung. Hat es geschneit, ist die Winterstimmung perfekt. Von der Aussichtsplattform auf St. Petri bietet sich dann ein romantischer Blick, der Schnee glättet den rauen Charme Lübecks in der dunklen Jahreszeit.

Once the Christmas market closes, the market square hosts an ice skating rink. A blanket of snow turns it into the perfect winter wonderland. The observation platform in the steeple of St. Petri Church offers romantic views, and the snow softens Lübeck's rough charm in the dark winter months.

KLARE KANTE / *MIRROR IMAGE*

Bunt strahlen die Häuser an der Obertrave. Auch in der Wintersonne. Und doppelt, wenn das Wasser der Trave ganz ruhig dahinfließt. Kann man sich vorstellen, dass hier eine vierspurige Straße verläuft? Stadtplaner der 1960er Jahre konnten es. Zum großen Glück verschwanden ihre Pläne erst in Amtsschubladen und dann im Archiv der Hansestadt Lübeck.

The colourful houses on the Upper Trave glisten in the winter sun. And even more so when reflected in the slow-moving waters of the Trave. Can you imagine a four-lane road in its place? City planners in the 1960s could. Fortunately, their plans disappeared into drawers and then into the archives of the Hanseatic City of Lübeck.

NORDISCHE HELLE / *NORDIC LIGHT*

Winterruhe an der Obertrave, so scheint es, doch in den Räumen der Musikhochschule in der Großen Petersgrube wird sicher geprobt. Vielleicht der Winter aus Vivaldis *Vier Jahreszeiten* oder Haydns *Jahreszeiten*. Oder Kantaten von Dieterich Buxtehude und Johann Sebastian Bach, die später in den Lübecker Kirchen zu hören sein werden.

A serene winter scene on the Upper Trave accompanied by the sound of students practising at the Academy of Music on the Grosse Petersgrube. Perhaps 'Winter' from Vivaldi's Four Seasons or Haydn's The Seasons. Or cantatas by Dieterich Buxtehude and Johann Sebastian Bach, to be performed later in Lübeck's churches.

EISZEIT / *ICE AGE*

In Lübecks Norden ist die Natur nicht zu beherrschen. Seit der letzten Eiszeit nagt die Ostsee an der Küste, frisst sich in das Steilufer und lässt es abbrechen. Jedes Jahr wird Lübeck hier ein bisschen kleiner, verliert Land an das Meer. So ist das nördlich von Travemünde gelegene Brodtener Ufer auch ein Sinnbild für die Verletzlichkeit der Natur. Aus menschlichem Ermessen ewig sind nur die Findlinge aus nordischem Gestein.

In the northern part of Lübeck, nature takes its course. Since the last ice age, the Baltic Sea has been gnawing away at the coastline, eating into the bluff, causing it to crumble. This part of Lübeck loses land to the sea every year. The Brodtener Ufer, the steep coastline north of Travemünde, is emblematic of the fragility of nature. Only the erratic boulders carried from the north by glaciers represent permanence in a human timescale.

INDEX

A
Altäre 20, 112-115, 146 f., 204
An der Mauer 85
Antiquariat 172 f.

B
Berkentienhaus 64 f.
Bibliothek der Hansestadt Lübeck 164-167
Bildende Kunst 20, 33, 48 f., 61-63, 78, 92 f., 112-115, 147, 169-172, 175, 187, 202-206
Böttcherstraße 43
Brodtener Ufer 218 f.
Brücken 180 f., 195
Bücher 162-167, 172 f.
Burgkloster 54, 120 f., 123
Burgtor 154 f., 178-180
Butendach-Bibliothek 162 f.

C
Clemensstraße 47

D
Domkirchhof 186 f.
Drehbrücke 181
Drehbrückenplatz 95, 140

E
Elbe-Lübeck-Kanal 183
Engelsgrube 144, 196

F
Fehmarnbelt, Feuerschiff 129, 134-139
Fleischhauerstraße 44
Füchtingshof 91

G
Galow, Florian 152 f.
Gänge 13, 86-89
Gewölbekeller 108 f.
Glandorps Hof 90
Glockengießerstraße 102 f.

Große Burgstraße 45
Große Petersgrube 50, 157, 216
Grün in der Stadt 56 f., 85-93, 96, 100, 182-188
Günter und Ute Grass Stiftung 170, 172

H
Hafenschuppen 94, 128 f., 134-142, 145, 180, 194, 208 f.
Handwerk 50 f., 65, 68 f., 101
Heiligen-Geist-Hospital 56 f., 206 f.
Holstentor 10, 176, 210
Hubbrücke 180 f., 195
Hüxstraße 36-41

K
Kanzleigebäude 46, 197
Karweick, Felix 92 f.
Kirchen
    Dom 16, 100 f., 183, 186-191, 198, 204 f., 211, 214 f.
    Herz-Jesu-Kirche 100, 122 f., 211
    Lutherkirche 122
    Reformierte Kirche 58 f., 108 f., 162 f.
    St. Aegidien 99, 150, 198-203
    St. Jakobi 54 f., 128, 133, 144-151, 164, 209
    St. Katharinen 102-107
    St. Marien 12, 16-23, 52, 98, 128, 204, 217
    St. Petri 10-16, 50, 53, 98, 156, 210, 217
Kirchenbauhütte 50 f.
Klatt, Frauke 78
Koberg 56 f.
Krähenteich 98 f., 182
Krane 128-133, 138, 140, 142
Kulturwerft Gollan 158 f.
Kunsthandwerk 66 f., 207
Kunsthaus Lübeck 170-173
Künstler und Künstlerinnen 48 f., 78, 92, 207
Kunsttankstelle Defacto Art 92 f.

L
Lisa von Lübeck, Kraweel 129, 142 f., 208
Literatur 160-173
Lübecker Märtyrer 122 f.

M
Marcks, Gerhard 20, 204
Markt 23 f., 212 f.
Max and Friends 130 f.
Mengstraße 42, 196
Moser, Maria 147
Mühlenteich 188 f.
Museen
    Buddenbrookhaus 160 f.
    Europäisches Hansemuseum 116-121, 123
    Günter Grass-Haus 168 f.
    Industriemuseum Geschichtswerkstatt Herrenwyk 126 f.
    Museum Behnhaus Drägerhaus 62 f., 174 f., 187
    Museum für Natur und Umwelt 190 f.
    Museum Holstentor 176 f.
    St. Annen-Museum 60 f., 112-115, 190
    Willy-Brandt-Haus 124 f.
    Museumshafen 94, 128, 134-137
Musik 45, 130 f., 152-159
Musikhochschule 156 f.

N
Nebel 192-195
Niederegger Marzipansalon 68 f.

O
Obertrave 12, 96-98, 100, 156 f., 214 f., 216 f.
Orgeln 19, 150 f.

P
Pamir, Rettungsboot 149
Passat, Viermastbark 72-75
Passathafen 72-75
Pastorenhäuser 55

Q
Querstraßen 42 f., 84 f., 193

R
Rathaus 22-35, 212 f.
Rathausarkaden 46, 197
Rosengarten 90
Rotter, Glasmanufaktur 66 f.

S
Salzspeicher 11, 97, 192, 211
Schabbelhaus 42
Schaufensterbummel 37-39
Schiffergesellschaft 70 f.
Schulgarten 184 f.
Siebente Querstraße 193
Skandinavienkai 76
Stadthafen 16, 94, 128-143, 145, 194 f.
Stadtmauer 99, 178 f.
Stiftungshöfe 90 f.
Strand 79-83, 218 f.
Strandsalon 130 f.
Synagoge 110 f.

T
Thierig, Bettina 48 f.
Tonfink 45
Travemünde 72-83, 218 f.

U
Untertrave 94 f., 128 f., 134-137, 140 f.

W
Waldzimmer 152 f.
Wallhalbinsel 130 f., 138-140, 142 f.
Weberstraße 84
Weihnachtsstadt 204-213
Wohnen 60-65

Z
Zeidler, Max 154 f.

KAREN MEYER-REBENTISCH
Dr. Karen Meyer-Rebentisch ist Fotografin, Autorin, Ausstellungsmacherin und Historikerin. Sie entschied sich 1993, nach Lübeck zu ziehen, und hat das noch keinen Tag bereut. Schwerpunkt ihrer fotografischen Arbeit sind die Stadt- und Reisefotografie sowie Gartenreportagen. www.meyer-rebentisch.de

Dr. Karen Meyer-Rebentisch is a photographer, author, exhibition organiser, and historian. In 1993, she decided to move to Lübeck, and has not regretted this decision for a moment. Her photographic work focuses on cities, travel and garden reports. www.meyer-rebentisch.de

JAN ZIMMERMANN
Dr. Jan Zimmermann lebt mal in Hamburg, mal in Lübeck. Er ist Autor, Historiker und betreibt die Bildagentur Vintage Germany. www.vintage-germany.de

Dr. Jan Zimmermann divides his time between Hamburg and Lübeck. He is a writer and historian, and runs the photo agency Vintage Germany. www.vintage-germany.de

Junius Verlag GmbH
Stresemannstraße 375
22761 Hamburg
www.junius-verlag.de

© 2021 by Junius Verlag GmbH
© für Fotografien: Karen Meyer-Rebentisch
© für Texte: Jan Zimmermann
© für Porträtfoto Karen Meyer-Rebentisch (S. 223): Sibylle Ostermann
© für Videoinstallation am Buddenbrookhaus (S. 160): Petar Florean, www.awforge.de
© für Kunstwerke: VG Bild-Kunst, Bonn 2021 (Christus von Gerhard Marcks in St. Marien,
S. 20 und 204; Überformung Ehrenmal von Maria Moser, S. 148)
Alle Rechte vorbehalten.

Übersetzung: Alexis Conklin & Stephen Roche, networktranslators.de
Gestaltung und Satz: Benjamin Wolbergs
Druck und Bindung: Grafisches Centrum Cuno GmbH & Co. KG

Karen Meyer-Rebentisch fotografiert mit einer Pentax-Kamera und Filtern von B+W.

Printed in Germany
1. Auflage 2021
ISBN 978-3-96060-544-7

Die Deutsche Nationalbibliothek verzeichnet diese Publikation in der Deutschen Nationalbibliografie;
detaillierte bibliografische Daten sind im Internet über http://dnb.dnb.de abrufbar.